THE ARTICULATE DEAD

The Articulate Dead

They Brought the Spirit World Alive

Michael Tymn

2015

Galde Press

Lakeville, Minnesota, U.S.A.

First Edition
Fourth Printing, 2015

Cover design by Christopher Wells

Cover illustration:
The spirit of Frank R. Stockton dictates to medium Etta De Camp.

Galde Press
PO Box 460
Lakeville, Minnesota 55044–0460
www.galdepress.com

For Gina

Death does not "do us part"

The decisive question for man is: Is he related to something infinite or not? That is the telling question of his life. Only if we know that the thing which truly matters is the infinite can we avoid fixing our interest upon futilities, and upon all kinds of goals which are not of real importance.

—**Carl G. Jung, M.D.**

As anyone may see on running through the series of Ingersoll lectures delivered annually for many years by distinguished philosophers, modern philosophy shows a strong tendency to burke this question [personality surviving death], to sit on the fence, or to assure us of immortality and survival in some sense that has neither interest nor significance for the plain man; in short, in some purely Pickwickian sense.

—**William McDougall, M.D.**

Healthy Skepticism is the basis of all accurate observation, but there comes a time when incredulity means either culpable ignorance or else imbecility; and this time has been long past in the matter of spirit intercourse.

—**Sir Arthur Conan Doyle, M.D.**

Perhaps it will be asked what benefit may be expected from a general acceptance of this evidence for survival. I think it will do for others what it has done for me. It has supplemented and reinforced my faith, both in times of bereavement and in the prospect of old age and death. Also, it has further emphasized the value of personal religion.

—**The Rev. Charles Drayton Thomas**

Contents

Foreword

As a scientist for most of my adult life, I rarely thought about mediums. When I did consider them, I thought they were fortunetellers or just plain charlatans. In 1997, after evaluating my near-death experience (NDE), I became interested in spirituality, religion and paranormal phenomena. This led to my joining the Academy of Spirituality and Paranormal Studies (ASPSI)*, becoming the editor of its journal, and writing *Searching for Eternity: A Scientist's Spiritual Journey to Overcome Death Anxiety*. In researching that book, I evaluated a variety of paranormal phenomena, including NDEs, out-of-body experiences (OBEs), apparitions, visions, dreams, mediumship, electronic voice phenomena, past life regressions, and other evidence for reincarnation. I concluded that the best evidence for a surviving soul, the existence of an afterlife, and the reality of God came from NDEs. I changed my previous belief about mediums and realized that although many were charlatans, there were a few who apparently did make contact with deceased entities. Nevertheless, even with those I was still not convinced of their veracity.

As a result of several submissions to *The Journal of Spirituality and Paranormal Studies* and from meetings of the Academy, plus watching popular mediums such as John Edward and James Van Praagh, I realized that there were a few current mediums who appeared to be authentic, and many more in the late 1800s through the mid-1900s who also seemed to have made contact with the deceased. However, I believed that those previous reports might have been deceptions because of the lack of good scientific investigations in those years. After reading the rough draft of this book I realized that I was wrong on both counts, i.e., scientific investigations and reliable medium contacts. There were several eminent scientists, such as Sir William Crookes, Sir Oliver Lodge, Dr. Alfred Russel Wallace, and Dr. Charles Richet who began as skeptics, but after thoroughly investigating mediums they became convinced that some were genuine. For them, the evidence appeared incontrovertible.

Why were there so many more medium reports in those days (and so many eminent scientists willing to examine the evidence) and so few medium reports currently with only a few scientists willing to investigate mediums? I believe the answer is that before movies, cable television, VHSs, DVDs, computers, the Internet, iPods, rapid air travel, and cell phones, scientists and people in general had a lot more free time and were willing to wait the lengthy time it often took for medium contacts to take place. It could be that it is difficult for discarnate spirits to make contact with us, and that is why it took so long for contact to be made in the past. Nowadays, with rapid mass communication and so much to do, most scientists and people in general do not have the time or patience to investigate mediums and wait for events to unfold. Many believe that today's science is so much better than that of the late 1800s to the mid-1900s that even apparently good investigations of mediums by eminent scientists of that era would not be reliable. However, after reading *The Articulate Dead* and discussing its conclusions with eminent current scientists, I am convinced that even had those previous scientists the use of modern technology they would have come to the same conclusions.

In a thoroughly enjoyable manner, Mike Tymn takes us back to that era when mediumship flourished. We accompany the scientists and the mediums as they divulge amazing results. It is difficult to remain a real skeptic after reading this outstanding book. Even though not everyone will be convinced that mediums can and do communicate with deceased entities, most people will come away from *The Articulate Dead* with a new appreciation and understanding of mediums and their uncanny abilities.

Donald R. Morse, DDS, Ph.D.

---

*Until January 1, 2006, the Academy of Spirituality and Paranormal Studies, Inc. (ASPSI) was known as the Academy of Religion and Psychical Research (ARPR). Its website is *http://www.aspsi.org*

Preface

This book resurrects some of the most interesting and credible personalities and cases in the annals of psychical research from the period 1850 to 1940, what might be called the "heyday" of mediumship, or spirit communication. I have intentionally avoided controversial cases, even where the preponderance of evidence was for them being genuine. And while several cases in this book were not subject to significant scientific investigation, I have included them based upon the apparent sincerity, reputation, and credibility of the authors and mediums along with the fact that the phenomena are consistent with those reported in the cases which were thoroughly investigated.

My purpose in resurrecting these old cases is to provide evidence of a spirit world—evidence that seems to have been forgotten or ignored—and, concomitantly, the survival of consciousness at death, i.e., an afterlife. As I was collecting the stories and writing the book during 2005, I watched three television specials having to do with the existence of God and/or the existence of an afterlife. Not one of them even alluded to the in-depth research and conclusions of the distinguished scholars and scientists you'll meet in this book. Religious leaders, skeptics, and atheists were allowed to voice their beliefs in each of the television programs, and in the end it came down to either accepting God and survival on blind faith or simply rejecting them because the evidence for them has not met strict scientific standards. There was often confusion among the moderators, panel members, and interviewees relative to the meanings of "evidence" and "proof." They were sometimes used interchangeably.

In our courts, we need only a preponderance of evidence to prove a case in a civil suit, meaning essentially that the evidence for outweighs the evidence against. In criminal cases, the standards are higher, requiring evidence that goes beyond a reasonable doubt. However, "reasonable doubt" does not mean *absolute* proof or no doubt at all. There are very few, if any, things subject to *absolute* proof. The point is that while there may not be absolute proof of survival, there is certainly some very strong evidence in favor of it. Most of the distinguished researchers mentioned in this book came away from their investigations convinced that the evidence at least met the "preponderance" standard, while many of them appear to have concluded that the evidence went "beyond a reasonable doubt." The debunkers can come up with all kinds of theories as to why the research was faulty, but those theories are usually nothing more than speculation. One modern debunker discredits the research of Professor Robert Hare, whom you'll meet in Chapter One, because Hare was seventy-three years old when he began investigating mediums. The debunker seems to have assumed that anyone that old must not be very observant and is easily duped. Other historians dismiss the research of the scholars and scientists who had the courage to commit themselves to the spirit and survival hypotheses, calling them "propagandists," as if to suggest that if a person is to remain objective and true to science he must "sit on the fence" all his life, never committing to anything. As the debunker appears to see it, once the researcher commits himself and becomes a "propagandist," all of his prior research is null and void.

No one denies that psychical research does not lend itself to the strict disciplines of laboratory science. Exact measurements, detailed testing, and replication are rarely possible when observing psychic phenomena. While scientists like to fit square pegs into square holes, psychical research usually involves trying to fit round pegs into square holes. Sometimes they fit, but gaps are left on the four corners, and such gaps cannot be tolerated by scientific fundamentalists.

After reading the rough draft of this book, a scientifically-minded friend opined that I had not offered enough of the skeptic's view of the various mediums and phenomena discussed. The comment reminded me of something Dr. Gary Schwartz, a University of Arizona researcher and author of *The Afterlife Experiments,* told me in an interview not long before. He noted that when television journalists reported on his research they presented it as if there are two sides—the medium and Schwartz vs. the debunking skeptic, who really knows little or nothing about the case. As Schwartz pointed out, there are, in fact, three sides—the medium, the skeptic, and the researcher, who should begin as a skeptic. The fact that the researcher is able to move away from his skepticism after thoroughly examining the case should not mean that a paid debunker must be called in to rescue science, but sadly that's the way it has been for many years. It is part of the reason, I believe, why the researchers, mediums, and cases mentioned in this book have been pretty much forgotten. With a skeptic or pseudoskeptic offering arguments already ruled out by the researcher (the former skeptic), the viewing audience sees it as a deadlock and doesn't know what to believe.

To my knowledge, none of the researchers who investigated Daniel Dunglas Home, William Stainton Moses, Leonora Piper, Gladys Osborne Leonard, and Pearl Curran, five mediums you'll read about in this book, ever accused them of fraud. In making that statement, I exclude scientists and scholars who may have only casually observed or just heard about them but were so certain such phenomena could not take place that they alleged fraud. I rely on the integrity of the respected researchers who observed the phenomena over and over again and then were willing to stake their reputations on validating them even when they knew their materialistic colleagues would smirk, snicker, and scoff. I'm referring to such esteemed researchers as Sir Oliver Lodge, Sir William Barrett, and Sir William Crookes, all men of honor, intelligence, and integrity knighted for their scientific discoveries outside of psychical research.

As Lodge, a physicist who did pioneering work in electricity and radio, saw it, any theory involving higher beings or spirits was likely to be extruded or discountenanced by scientists as a relic of primitive superstition, coming down from times when such infantile explanations were prevalent. This resistance by mainstream science was discussed more recently by Dr. John O'M. Bockris, a distinguished professor of science at Texas A & M University before his retirement in 1997. As he sees it, scientists, especially those in universities, reject all evidence for the paranormal as they are locked into the scientific paradigm and are "horrified to learn that they may not have been speaking the truth." (Brockris, 2005) He blames these closed-minded scientists for leading many in the West to approach death without hope, thereby giving rise to a more materialistic and hedonistic world. Dr. Neal Grossman, a professor of philosophy at the University of Illinois, says much the same thing about academic philosophers. That is, they "matriculate within a paradigm that is largely atheistic, materialistic, and reductionistic." (Grossman, 2002) Once they internalize that paradigm and become anchored in it, they are convinced that those operating out of a different paradigm must certainly be out of touch with reality.

In his 2003 book, *Pseudoscience* and *The Paranormal*, Terence Hines, a professor of psychology at Pace University, claims that there is not a shred of evidence for survival. He calls psychical research *pseudoscience*. His view is typical of the "skeptics" locked into the paradigm referred to by Bockris and Grossman. While Hines provides a bibliography of more than 500 references, he either ignorantly or conveniently avoids books by Lodge, Barrett, Crookes, and other reputable scientists and scholars. He does mention Robert Hare and Alfred Russel Wallace, but he dismisses their research with a remark that they were operating outside their areas of expertise. At the same time, he calls upon a far-fetched debunking theory by Michael Faraday to support his views, even though Faraday was equally outside his area of expertise and apparently had much less exposure to mediumistic phenomena than either Wallace or Hare.

As I see it, most of those wearing the "skeptic" badge are really *pseudoskeptics*. They are the fundamentalists of science and are as closed-minded as the fundamentalists of religion. They can pick holes here and there in all of the stories in this book. As previously stated, it is not an exact science and the researchers themselves were rarely totally convinced by any one case. What convinced most of them was the cumulative evidence of the many cases. It was one thing to have doubts about certain things in a particular case, but quite something else to doubt the same phenomenon occurring over and over again in hundreds of cases.

Once the fundamentalist of science is stuck in the paradigm with other members of academia, he or she takes on a certain intellectual arrogance. That bolstered ego may satisfy him until he is in the final stages of earthly life and awakens to his belief that he is, as C. G. Jung once put it, "marching toward nothingness." (Jung, 1961)

What the esteemed researchers involved in the cases in this book differed on was the interpretation of the phenomena. They struggled with whether the phenomena resulted from spirits or from some not-yet-understood psychological pathology. Many of the early researchers theorized that the mediums had a secondary personality buried away in the subconscious and that this secondary personality, unbeknownst to the primary personality, had mind-reading ability. When information came through that was unknown to the person sitting with the medium, i.e., outside direct telepathy, the theory was expanded to include mind-reading at a distance, or superESP, meaning that the secondary personality could tap into minds anywhere in the world, immediately process the information, and give prompt feedback to the sitter. It was as if there were a giant computer in the ethers which the medium could plug into. Some of these theories seem more fantastic than the spirit and survival hypotheses. The biggest blow to the telepathy and superESP theories came from the communication of George Pellew through Leonora Piper, as discussed in Chapter Eight.

The title of this book, *The Articulate Dead*, is based upon my observation that spirits communicating through mediums during the period 1850 to 1940 seemed to have had much more to say and better ways of saying it than spirits today do. I should probably say "the purported spirits," but, after many years of studying the subject I am satisfied beyond a reasonable doubt that these stories do involve actual spirit communication. Either that or the communicating spirit is some component of the "Higher Self" that is for the most part beyond human comprehension. One way or the other, the survival of individual consciousness at death is indicated.

There are two general types of communication coming from mediums, one referred to as "circular" and the other as "spiraling." In the former, the communication is pretty much limited to simple messages of identity and continued existence. It usually comes from spirits who have recently crossed over and want to let their loved ones know that they are still around. The spiraling type of mediumship involves more profound messages and comes from spirits more advanced or evolved.* Indications are, however, that some not-so-advanced spirits think they know more than they actually do and what they say is taken as "higher truth" simply because it is coming from the spirit world. As discussed below, we must "test" and "discern" the messages.

The skeptic might very well conclude that the decline in the quality of mediumship suggested by the title means that all of those old mediums were charlatans of one kind or another. Why else would there not be such stories

---

*This is now more often referred to as "channeling." See Glossary, Appendix A.

today? Several theories addressing that question will be discussed in the Epilogue.

Having briefly discussed the fundamentalists of science, I should also touch upon the fundamentalists of religion. It would seem that orthodox religions would have welcomed mediumship as supporting their basic tenets, but instead religious leaders strongly condemned it. They cited Old Testament passages such as Deuteronomy 18:12, which supposedly says that we should not speak with the dead, and Ecclesiastes 9:5, which suggests that the "dead know nothing." They ignored New Testament passages, such as 1 John 4:1, which says not to believe every spirit but to test them whether they are of God, 1 Corinthians 12:7–10, which states that some are given the gift of discerning the spirit messages, and Acts 2:17–18, where we are told that "your sons and daughters shall prophesy, and your young men shall see visions…"

As with so many other passages in the Bible, one can give various interpretations to them. It is impossible, however, to "test" and "discern" the messages if we don't listen to them. And, if the dead know nothing, why would we *bother* listening? If we are to strictly interpret Deuteronomy, then we must stone to death stubborn and rebellious children (21:18–21), accept polygamy (21:15), and put to death people in adulterous relationships (22:22).

It has been pointed out by a number of Bible scholars that the Old Testament prohibitions against communicating with the dead are misunderstood because what modern English versions now give as the word "dead" meant "spiritually dead" in the original Aramaic and Hebrew, referring to low-level or earthbound spirits, those orthodox religion says are in "hell." Revelation coming to us through modern mediumship suggests that such earthbound spirits do exist and some of them are as evil and devious as they were in their earth lives. Thus, there is good reason for warnings against communicating with spirits, as not everyone is able to "discern" the messages. But that certainly doesn't mean that we should ignore or avoid modern spirit messages. Nor does 1 Corinthians 12:7–10 suggest that the gift of discernment is given only to the priesthood.

Resistance by orthodox religion no doubt results from the fact that some of the messages coming through mediums seemingly contradict or conflict with established dogma and doctrine, thereby threatening the authority of church leadership. Rather than attempt to examine earlier interpretations given to passages in the Bible and other holy books, then test and discern the modern messages, the religious leaders have found it easier to simply condemn all of it as the work of Satan, completely overlooking the fact that much of what they now preach came to us through mediumship of one kind or another.* If they were to closely examine the newer messages, they would realize that the basic teachings of Jesus—*Love thy neighbor...*, *Do unto others...*, and *You reap what you sow*—are also teachings of both spiraling mediumship and the near-death experience. Moreover, many of the messages pay homage to Jesus. With proper testing and discernment, numerous new teachings edify and clarify Scripture, offering us language that is not muddled and befuddled by human hands and brains.

Clearly, we live in an era of moral decadence, a time of egocentricity, intolerance, hatred, hypocrisy, disorder, flux, strife, chaos, and fear. We have become hedonistic materialists, consumed with the pursuit of pleasure and sensory gratification, making merry with intoxicants and drugs, and reveling in the "Playboy" philosophy. Can any thinking person doubt that today's hedonistic materialism is a result of a loss of spiritual values, especially a lack of belief in survival? Can there be any other reason for it? Ponder on Dr. Jung's comment on the epigraph page preceding this Preface. The eminent Swiss psychiatrist also said that it is psychologically beneficial to have

---

*For example, the Ten Commandments appear to have ben given to Moses (a medium) by means of direct writing (Exodus 31:18, 34:1). In Rev. 1:10 and 4:1, we read of a voice coming from a trumpet, or direct-voice mediumship. In 1 Chronicles 28:19 and 2 Chronicles 26:12, we have what appears to be automatic writing. (See Appendix A for an explanation of the various types of mediumship.) There are a number of Bible passages mentioning angels speaking. These might very well have been translated "spirits comminicating."

death as a goal toward which to strive. Mozart called death the key to unlocking the door to true happiness. Shakespeare wrote that when we are prepared for death, life is sweeter. French philosopher Michel de Montaigne said that "to practice death is to practice freedom."

By no means were any of these great men saying that we should forget this life and live for a future one. They were saying that once we understand that death is a mere transition to a "larger life" we can see at least a little of the big picture and better live this one. Blind faith doesn't provide that understanding for most people. They need conviction—a conviction that comes from psychical research of the type covered in this book.

As a life-long Christian—although by no means an orthodox one—I have been able to advance from the blind faith asked of believers by church leaders to true faith, or conviction, based on my studies of these cases and others. There is much I don't understand and will never understand in this lifetime, but the cases summarized in this book have provided a peace of mind in my old age that religion could not. Moreover, so many of the confusing and perplexing things I was taught as a young Catholic now make perfect sense.

It is not an easy subject to comprehend. Perhaps the biggest obstacle to understanding some of the spirit communication, i.e., mediumship, related in this book is grasping the role and function of the so-called "spirit control," such as Leonora Piper's *Phinuit* and Gladys Osborne Leonard's *Feda*. I recommend that the reader spend a few minutes on the explanation of the spirit control in the glossary (Appendix A) before reading the stories involving spirit controls.

Introduction

Communication with the spirit world of God has been taking place for at least as long as recorded history, probably since the first humans inhabited the earth. The Bible is filled with stories of spirit communication, although modern translations usually refer to spirits as angels, messengers, or the Holy Ghost, and to the mediums as prophets. But a new era in spirit communication was triggered by an event that took place on March 31, 1848, at the small home of the John D. Fox family in Hydesville, New York, not far from Rochester.

Shortly after moving into the house on December 11, 1847, the family of four, including daughters Margaret, fourteen, and Kate, eight, began hearing strange raps and taps, but it wasn't until March 31 that the two daughters realized that they could communicate with the "raps" by snapping their fingers. Upon learning of this, Mrs. Fox asked the "raps" to respond to questions by giving two raps for a "yes" and silence for "no." She asked if a human being was making the raps. There was no response. When she asked, "Is it a spirit?" there were two raps. Neighbors were called in and dozens of questions were put to the "spirit." It was determined that the communicating spirit had been murdered in the house about five years earlier, before the Fox family moved in.

The questioning by this primitive method went on for days and it was further determined that the communicating spirit's body had been buried beneath the house. Digging began and at a depth of five feet human hair and bones were found.* It was soon realized that the Fox sisters were mediums and were thus able to bring through other spirits. Some amazing phenomena produced by their spirit controls** were witnessed by a number of eminent men and women, including Horace Greeley, J. Fenimore Cooper, and William Cullen Bryant. However, those stories are not part of this book, as the credibility of the sisters was compromised after they were turned into a sideshow act by P. T. Barnum, the showman. With audiences paying money to see them perform, they apparently turned to trickery when their powers failed them. After being convinced by religious fundamentalists that she was being used by the devil, Margaret, who had become an alcoholic and was suffering financially, told the *New York Herald* in an interview that she had resorted to fraud. She later repudiated the confession, stating that she needed money and was paid for the interview. Thus, the Fox sisters have gone down in many of the history books as outright frauds, when, in fact, they were likely "mixed mediums"—able to produce real phenomena at times but resorting to fraud at other times.† Such was also the plight of Italy's Eusapia

---

*An underground stream prevented further digging, but in 1904, fifty-six years later, more excavation was done and a complete skeleton was found, although there was a rumor that the skeleton was planted there by a prankster. As one delves into psychical research, he or she comes to realize that there is almost always some other story countering what at first seems to be factual. Indications are that many of these countering stories begin as rumors by sketics and then become part of the total story many years later. Thus, it becomes difficult to separate fact from fiction.

**See Appendix A for a definition of "spirit control."

†Clearly, mediums are not necessarily highly evoved souls or "saints." Some have been very good people, others of questionable character. Whatever physical anomaly exists to permit this "second sight," it is not selective.

Palladino, called by some researchers the greatest physical medium of her time. She was investigated by a dozen or more eminent scientists and scholars, all of whom were convinced that the phenomena they had observed, including spirit materializations, were genuine. Yet, they recognized that when her powers failed, she attempted to trick them. The attempted tricks did not produce any major phenomena, but they did affect her credibility. That there have been mixed mediums and outright charlatans is clear, but it is equally clear that there have been genuine mediums that did not resort to fraud. These are the mediums you'll read about in this book.

In spite of limited mass communications in those days, the Hydesville story quickly spread and turned into an epidemic of spirit communication. Mediums began developing in all parts of the United States as well as in Europe as the phenomena progressed from rappings and tappings to table tilting and turning and even table levitations. The table phenomena usually involved sitters placing their hands on the table and the table lifting off the floor, although there were many observations of the table tilting, turning, or lifting independently of any hands. The spirit communicator would then respond to questions by tilts of the table. In addition to the simple "yes" and "no" method employed in the Fox case, spirits would tap out letters of the alphabet (one tap for "A," five taps for "E," etc.) or would respond with a tap when the alphabet was recited by someone present, thereby slowly spelling out words and sentences. The "madness" came to be called "spiritualism."*

If the spirits who communicated in the years immediately following the Hydesville event are to be believed, there was a plan behind it all—a plan that resulted from a growing loss of faith and spiritual values in an increasingly materialistic world. "It is to draw mankind together in harmony, and

---

*Spiritualism in its broadest sense simply means the belief in a spirit world and communication with the spirits. In a more limited sense, it refers to organized religious groups calling themselves spiritualists. Not all spiritualists have exactly the same beliefs. While all believe in spirit communication, the main differences have to do with the role of Jesus in the spirit world and with reincarnation.

to convince skeptics of the immortality of the soul," was the reply given to Territory of Wisconsin Governor Nathaniel P. Tallmadge when he asked a communicating spirit claiming to be John C. Calhoun, a former vice-president of the United States, about the purpose of the strange phenomena. (Harding, 1970)

A few years before the Hydesville event in 1848, Andrew Jackson Davis, a young New York man born in 1826, began receiving profound messages purportedly coming from advanced spirits, but few paid any attention to him until after the epidemic was underway. Numerous books of wisdom flowed from the pen of this uneducated man, who came to be known as "the Poughkeepsie seer." Some years passed before an entry was discovered in Davis's journal for March 31, 1848. It read: "About daylight this morning a warm breathing passed over my face and I heard a voice, tender and strong, saying 'Brother, the good work has begun—behold a living demonstration is born.' I was left wondering what could be meant by such a message." (Doyle, 1926)

According to spirit messages received by the Rev. William Stainton Moses, the subject of Chapter Four, some two decades later, the rapping method was invented by Benjamin Franklin and Emanuel Swedenborg working together in the spirit world. It was pointed out that in the old days spirits communicated with men in ways less material, but as men grew more corporeal it became necessary for a material system of telegraphy to be invented. It also became increasingly clear that our spirit friends have as many obstacles to overcome in communicating with us as we have in communicating with them.

Andrew Jackson Davis.

Part I

Chapters 1 – 6

The Earliest Psychical Researchers

I found I had done a great wrong to men who had proclaimed new truths at the risk of their positions. When I remember that I branded as a fool that fearless investigator, Crookes, the inventor of the radiometer, because he had the courage to assert the reality of psychic phenomena and to subject them to scientific tests, and when I also recollect that I used to read his articles thereon in the same stupid style, regarding him as crazy, I am ashamed, both of myself and others, and I cry from the very bottom of my heart. "Father, I have sinned against the Light."

— **Dr. Julian Ochorowicz** (1850-1917)
Professor of psychology at the University of Warsaw

John W. Edmonds.

One

Early Critics Become Defenders and Martyrs

I found that there were many ways in which this unseen intelligence communed with us, besides his rappings and table tipping, and that through those other modes there came very many communications distinguished for their eloquence, their high order of intellect, and their pure moral tone.

—Judge John W. Edmonds

A highly-respected judge, a popular politician, and two renowned scientists were among the many intelligent and influential Americans who smirked, scoffed, and sneered at the mediumistic phenomena that had become an epidemic in the United States and Europe beginning in 1848. And yet, all four of these men became converts, defenders, and even martyrs.

Following the death of his wife, John W. Edmonds, Chief Justice of the New York State Supreme Court, was persuaded during January 1851 to attend a séance with friends. In an August 1, 1853, letter "to the public" released to various New York newspapers, he wrote that he attended thinking it fraud and intending to expose it as such. "Having from my researches come to a different conclusion, I feel that the obligation to make known the result is just as strong," he explained. "Therefore it is, mainly, because there is another consideration which influences me, and that is the desire to extend to others a knowledge which I am conscious cannot but make them happier and better" (Harding 1970).

Edmonds had served in both branches of the New York legislature, for some time as president of the Senate, before he was appointed to the Supreme Court. He had a reputation as a tough, scholarly, reform-minded lawyer. After witnessing phenomena that puzzled him in his first séance, Edmonds decided to investigate further. He later wrote that over a period of 23 months he witnessed several hundred manifestations in various forms, keeping very detailed records of them, collecting some 1,600 pages of manuscript. "I resorted to every expedient I could devise to detect imposture and to guard against delusion," Edmonds later wrote in a series of articles for the *New York Tribune.* "I felt in myself, and saw in others, how exciting was the idea that we were actually communing with the dead, and I laboured to prevent any undue bias of my judgment. I was at times critical and captious to an unreasonable extreme" (Wallace 1975).

Edmonds said that the manifestations were of almost every known form, both physical and mental. He observed a mahogany table with a lamp burning on it levitated at least a foot off the floor. He also observed a mahogany chair thrown on its side and moved swiftly back and forth on the floor with no one touching it. It repeatedly stopped abruptly within a few inches of him. As for spirit communications, there were many, the chief communicators being Swedenborg and Bacon. "I have heard the mediums use Greek, Latin, Spanish, and French words, when I knew they had no knowledge of any language but their own," Edmonds further recorded, "and it is a fact that can be attested to by many, that often there has been speaking and writing in foreign languages and unknown tongues by those who were unacquainted with either" (Harding 1970).

Edmonds became convinced that the cognate nature of much of the phenomena was evidence that there was a high order of intelligence involved—"an intelligence outside of, and beyond, mere mortal agency; for there was no other hypothesis which I could devise or hear of, that could at all explain [it]" (Harding 1970).

But Edmonds wondered what the purpose of it was. *Cui bono*—for what good? To what end? Why raps, taps, flying furniture, levitated humans, floating bells, and other seemingly ridiculous physical phenomena? Was it simply some form of amusement by low-level spirits? No, Edmonds concluded, there was clearly a purpose behind it. Those in the spirit world had recently learned how to contact us and were making their existence known in whatever way they could. Their purpose was to let us know they were there, to give us hope, to help us overcome our doubts and diminishing faith in an age of reason.

Sometime in 1853, Edmonds discovered that he had mediumistic abilities and began receiving messages by means of automatic writing. He recalled receiving a spirit message early one morning that his grandson, some 400 miles away, was seriously sick. He immediately traveled there and found his grandson recovering, but his daughter informed him that at the time the message was received the boy was very sick.

But it was Edmonds's daughter, Laura, who really had the gift of mediumship. She developed into a trance medium. It was reported that although she knew only English and a smattering of French in her awakened state, she spoke Spanish, French, Greek, Italian, Portuguese, Latin, Hungarian, and Indian dialects fluently when entranced (or rather the spirits spoke the languages using her voice mechanism). Edmonds wrote that a Mr. E. D. Green, an artist of his city, came for a sitting with his daughter accompanied by an acquaintance from Greece. While the man from Greece spoke entirely in Greek for more than an hour, the replies coming through his daughter were sometimes in Greek and sometimes in English.

After writing a book on his experiences with mediums, Edmonds came under attack by politicians, the press, and the pulpit, and was forced to resign his position on the Supreme Court, returning to the practice of law. "The publication of a book on spiritualism by a person so distinguished as Judge Edmonds, of our Supreme Court, is an event in literature demanding more than a passing notice," an objective editorial in the December 1853 edition of *Putnam's Monthly* read. "The subject and the author alike arrest the public attention. An attempt to prove the reality of an intercourse between departed spirits and men on this side of the grave, by an eminent judicial functionary, is a fact that has much significance." The editorial went on to say that a large number of people of different ages and conditions in the United States, England, France, Austria, Central America, and India had reported curious phenomena, such as rappings, table-turnings, bell-ringings, poundings, and writings in recent years and that there was much similarity in the reports. "The reputation of such an endorser as Judge Edmonds—a lawyer of great sagacity, accustomed to weighing evidence, and a man of the most exemplary integrity, whose words on a matter of fact cannot be doubted—ought to commend the subject to an impartial investigation, or at least shield it from flippant commentaries on the lower order of journalism."

Among those standing to defend Judge Edmonds was Territory of Wisconsin Governor Nathaniel P. Tallmadge, a former New York senator who had been associated with Edmonds in the New York legislature. Tallmadge said that before he became aware of Edmonds's interest in spiritualistic phenomena he had heard of the "Rochester knockings" involving the Fox sisters, but he had paid no heed to them. Rather, he considered them a delusion that would soon pass away. However, after Edmonds made his beliefs known, Tallmadge felt that it was at least a subject worthy of investigation.

At sittings with a number of mediums, Tallmadge received communications purporting to come from the spirit of his old friend, John C. Calhoun, a former vice-president of the United States who had died in 1850. "They have been received through rapping, writing, and speaking mediums, and are of the most extraordinary character," Tallmadge wrote in a letter to

Helen N. Whitman, a celebrated poet from Rhode Island (Harding 1970). After a message that came through direct-writing (a pencil was held by an invisible hand),* Tallmadge found it to be "a perfect facsimile of the handwriting of John C. Calhoun." He took the message to General and Mrs. Hamilton, who had many private letters from Calhoun. They too pronounced it to be Calhoun's handwriting and further commented that the terse style was very much Calhoun's, including the fact that he always used the contraction "I'm" rather than writing "I am," as was more common then.

Like Edmonds, Tallmadge wondered about the purpose of the communication and asked Calhoun to explain. "It is to draw mankind together in harmony, and convince skeptics of the immortality of the soul," Calhoun responded (Harding 1970).

At a sitting with Margaret and Kate Fox, Tallmadge, General Hamilton, and General Waddy Thompson were directed by Calhoun by means of the slow rapping method (one rap for each letter of the alphabet) to go to the Bible and read St. John's Gospel, third chapter, verses 8, 11, 19, and 34. They did so and found:

Verse 8: "The wind bloweth where it will, and thou hearest its voice, but knowest not whence it cometh or whither it goeth; so is every one that is born of the spirit."

Verse 11: "Verily, verily I say unto thee, we speak what we know and testify what we have seen, and ye receive not our testimony."

Verse 19: "And this is the condemnation, that light is come into the world, and men love darkness rather than light because their deeds are evil."

Verse 34: "For he whom God hath sent speaketh the words of God; for God giveth not the spirit by measure" (Harding 1970).

Meanwhile, in a letter dated July 27, 1853, to the *Philadelphia Inquirer,* Dr. Robert Hare, emeritus professor of chemistry at the University of Pennsylvania, denounced the "popular madness" being called "spiritualism" by

---

*See Appendix A for a further explanation of "direct writing."

Robert Hare.

the American press. He claimed that the phenomena of raps, taps, tilting, turning, and levitating of tables purportedly bringing messages from the dead were either unconscious muscular actions on the part of the persons with whom the phenomena were associated or hallucinations.

The author of more than 150 papers on scientific subjects, Hare was also a world-renowned inventor, his best-known invention being the oxyhydrogen blowpipe, a forerunner of the modern welding torch. He was awarded honorary M. D. degrees by both Yale and Harvard and was an associate of the Smithsonian Institute as well as many other scientific organizations. He considered it his moral duty as a scientist to expose spiritualism as just so much flimflam.

But shortly after Hare's letter appeared in the *Inquirer*, he received a letter from one Amasa Holcombe, apparently an educated person who had shared Hare's view before observing some of the phenomena. Holcombe discreetly challenged Hare to make a scientific investigation and not just assume that it was all fraudulent. Hare agreed that it was the proper thing to do. Apparently, it didn't take long for him to change his mind. "I sincerely believe that I have communicated with the spirits of my parents, sister, brother, and dearest friends, and likewise with the spirits of the illustrious Washington and other worthies of the spirit world; that I am by them commissioned, under their auspices, to teach truth and to expose error," Hare wrote, as he completely recanted his earlier statements, admitting that he had not properly investigated the phenomena and simply assumed they could not be true as they were contrary—or at least seemed so—to the laws of science.

"In common with almost all educated persons of the nineteenth century, I had been brought up deaf to any testimony which claimed assistance from supernatural causes, such as ghosts, magic, or witchcraft," Hare explained his earlier position (Hare 1855).

Sitting with a number of mediums but particularly a Mrs. M. B. Gourlay, Hare was frustrated at the slowness in the communication process and proceeded to invent several instruments designed to facilitate the process. One of these instruments was somehow connected to the tilting table to rapidly record the communication. Another, called a "spiritscope," had a rotating disk with letters and numbers on it and was operated with levers and pulleys, a mechanical forerunner of the Ouija board. A medium would sit on one side of the instrument, blind to the side with the letters and numbers, as the spirit communicator manipulated the device through her hands.

During one of his early sittings, Hare observed a table levitate and move about the room. He fully examined it to rule out any kind of invisible wires. One of the communicators was Hare's deceased father, also named Robert, an English emigrant who established a large brewery in Philadelphia. "Oh, my son, listen to reason!" the father told his then still-skeptical son (Hare 1855). Many others, including his mother and sister, also communicated. Questions were answered and evidence provided—all outside the scope of research by the medium—to eventually win Hare over to a belief in the reality of spiritualism.

According to the senior Hare, the phenomena of spiritualism was "a deliberate effort on the part of the inhabitants of the higher spheres to break through the partition which has interfered with the attainment, by mortals, of a correct idea of their destiny after death." (Hare 1855) He further explained to his son that a delegation of advanced spirits had been appointed for the project, the ultimate goal being to replace blind faith with a positive philosophy. "It will expand and liberalize the mind far beyond your present conceptions," the senior Hare communicated. "It will fraternize and unite all the members of the human family in an everlasting bond of spiritual union and harmonial brotherhood. It will establish the principles of love to God and your fellows. It will do away with sectarian bigotry. It will show that so many of the so-called religious teachings are but impositions on the credulity of mankind, being founded on the grossest absurdities and palpable ignorance of the nature of things. It will give man higher and infinitely more exalted views of God, and bring him into closer communion with the Author

Robert Hare's spiritscope.

of his being. It will do away completely with the sting of death, and rob the grave of its terrors" (Hare 1855).

The incarnate Hare asked his father why low spirits were allowed to interfere in the undertaking, mentioning a case where there was mischievous displacement of furniture by the spirits. The father explained that the spirits in the lower spheres are better able to make mechanical movements and loud rappings, and thus their assistance was required. The raps, he further explained, were produced by voluntary discharges of the vitalized spiritual electricity from the spirit coming in contact with the animal electricity emanating from the medium. The spirits were able to direct these discharges at will to any particular locality, thereby producing sounds or concussion. It was also mentioned that things such as the levitation of tables, which did not involve communication, were simply to get attention and create interest.

As for using the hand of the medium, as in automatic writing, it was explained that the spirits direct currents of vitalized spiritual electricity on the particular muscles which they desire to control. It is not necessary that the medium be a person of good moral character or have a well-balanced mind, but an advanced spirit would not be able to control the organs or mind of a medium unless in affinity with the medium. When spirits wish to impress the mind of the medium, the spirits can dispose and arrange the magnetic currents of the brain so as to form or fashion them into ideas of their own. They can instantly determine the sphere of a spirit, in or out of the body, by the particular brilliancy and character of the light in which he or she is enveloped, as well as by the peculiar sensation which his or her presence creates.

Hare asked his father why Hydesville was selected as the place to launch this project. His father replied that the spirit of a murdered man would excite more interest and that it was necessary to use a community where spiritual agency would be more readily credited than one where the more-educated would be prejudiced against it and dismiss it as delusion.

After being convinced that he was indeed in touch with the "dead," Hare began to request information as to their abodes, their modes of existence, and their theological doctrines. He was told by his father that habitation is divided into seven concentric regions called spheres. The sphere closest to earth—the one we in the flesh occupy—is known as the first or rudimental sphere. The remaining six are the spiritual spheres. Evil or misdirected spirits find their affinities in the second sphere and remain there for an indefinite period of time, enveloped in darkness and in moral depravity. Through the benign influence exerted by higher intelligences, the grosser passions of these earthbound spirits, sooner or later, begin to subside and they gradually aspire to higher associations and circumstances.

The social constitution of the spheres, according to the senior Hare, is divided into six circles, or societies, in which kindred and congenial spirits are united and subsist together based on the law of affinity. When a spirit sheds the flesh, it enters the sphere and circle for which it is morally and intellectually adapted. Those who are related in the flesh may or may not be linked together on a particular sphere based on the affinity they have for each other as well as their moral and intellectual adaptation. Still, they may occasionally meet with each other, those in the higher spheres passing to the lower to visit. Those in the lower spheres never ascend to the higher until fully prepared for such a transition based on the laws of progression. Each society has teachers from the spheres above. By receiving and giving knowledge, our moral and intellectual faculties are expanded to higher conceptions and more exalted views of the great Creator.

There is no division of time into days, weeks, months, or years, it was further explained. "Although we, like you, are constantly progressing toward perfection, our ideas of time and the seasons differ widely from yours," the senior Hare continued. "With you, it is time—with us, eternity. In the terrestrial sphere, a man's thoughts, being bounded by time and space, are limited; but with us they are extended in proportion as we get rid of those restrictions and our perception of truth becomes more accurate" (Hare 1855).

Hare became acquainted with a spirit named Maria, the deceased daughter of a personal friend. Hare accompanied the friend to a sitting with Mrs. Gourlay when Maria communicated, giving details of her awakening in her new environment. "I felt like one just awakening from a deep sleep induced by the deadening influence of an opiate," she recalled. "It was some time before I could collect my scattered senses. On partially regaining my consciousness, I recollected having been sick, and the anxiety of my friends for my restoration to health; and I wondered at the sudden change in my feelings. Those racking pains I experienced had all fled, and I felt a newness of life which was truly delightful. Indistinct and shadowy forms flitted before me. On closely inspecting them, I perceived that they were my departed friends. It was then that I fully realized the change in my condition" (Hare 1855).

Maria went on to say that her first concern was for the grief felt by loved ones left behind. As her vision became clearer, she recognized her brother William ready to receive her. Clothed in a garment of living light,

William welcomed her and told her that he had been her guardian angel through life. After other deceased friends and relatives greeted her, William accompanied her into the second sphere, where there was moral darkness pervading the atmosphere, rendering it a gloomy and uncomfortable in the extreme. The inhabitants there appeared dark and dismal and seemed to be continually tortured with the pangs of a guilty conscience. There was much disorder and confusion.

On passing into the third sphere, they were met by a company of angels from the seventh sphere, among them a brother who had died in infancy. Compared with the second sphere, there was order in the third sphere, the beauty of which transcends that of earth. "The scenery is endlessly diversified with spiritual objects, corresponding to things of your planet," she communicated. "Mountains and valleys, hills and dales, rivers and lakes, and trees and plants, lend their enchantment to the scene." She went on to say that the inhabitants of this sphere are anxious for instruction and she observed a class in which spirits were intently listening to a teacher speaking on the subject of progression.

They continued on into the fourth sphere, which Maria described as "an enchanted land" filled with flowers and rapturous strains of music. They visited a beautiful temple devoted to the science of the harmony of sounds. There she saw many "master spirits of song" who lived ages ago on earth, attuning their instruments to harmony. Maria perceived that the fourth sphere was to be her abiding place for the present. However, she later returned to the second sphere to further observe, finding it less frightening this time. "Its denizens are seen straggling here and there, with no fixed object in view," she related. "All are seeking to minister to their perverted tastes. Some are holding forth in loud tones, and painting in false and gaudy colors the joy of their home; others, who occupied high stations on earth, hang their heads in confusion, and would fain hide themselves from view" (Hare 1855).

At some point in time, Hare realized that he had mediumistic powers and no longer required the help of other mediums. "It is now my own character only that can be in question," he wrote (Hare 1855).

"It is a well-known saying that there is 'but one step between the sublime and the ridiculous,'" Hare summed up his new philosophy, fully aware that many of his scientific peers were then deriding him. "This idea was never verified more fully than in the position I find myself now occupying, accordingly as those by whom that position is viewed may consider the manifestations which have given rise to it in the light wherein they are now viewed by me, *or as they were two years ago viewed by myself, and are now seen* by the great majority of my estimable contemporaries" (Hare 1855).

Another distinguished scientist converted to spiritualism after setting out to rescue his friends who were "running to mental seed and imbecility" over the mediumistic phenomena was James J. Mapes, a professor of chemistry and natural philosophy at the National Academy of Design in New York as well as a renowned inventor of agricultural products. In fact, Mapes's daughter had become a writing medium. When Mapes asked her to demonstrate her powers to him, she took a pen and wrote a message that appeared to come from Mapes's father. When Mapes asked for proof of identity, his daughter's hand wrote: "You may recollect that I gave you, among other books, an encyclopedia; look at page 120 of that book, and you will find my name written there, which you have seen" (Doyle 1926). Mapes had not seen the book for twenty-seven years as it had been stored in a warehouse. He retrieved it and found his father's name written on page 120. After sitting with various other mediums, Mapes wrote: "The manifestations which are pertinent to the ends required are so conclusive in their character as to establish in my mind certain cardinal points. These are: First, there is a future state of existence, which is but a continuation of our present state of being…Second, that the great aim of nature, as shown through a great variety of spiritual existences is progression, extending beyond the limits of this mundane sphere…Third, that spirits can and do communicate with mortals, and in all cases evince a desire to elevate and advance those they commune with" (Harding 1970).

While Edmonds, Tallmadge, Hare, and Mapes all became converts by means of constant observation, Leo Miller, a young New York lawyer, experienced a totally different kind of conversion. Described as an eloquent and attractive speaker, Miller began giving public lectures in which he attempted to explain the deceptions of spiritualism, pointing out that all the raps and taps were nothing more than mediums cracking their knee, ankle, and toe joints while otherwise engaged in fraud. However, in one such lecture, Miller thoroughly confused his audience when he went into a trance and began speaking in favor of the phenomena. Returning home perplexed and bewildered, Miller began experiencing raps and then voices of invisible beings rebuking him for his past perversity and urging him to make amends by going forth and proclaiming the truth, instructions which Miller heeded.

Two

The Epidemic Hits France

Let those who scoff at the idea of spirit teachings give us a nobler idea than is given by those teachings of the handiwork of God, a more convincing denomination of His goodness and His power.

—**Allan Kardec**

The spiritualism craze ignited by the strange rappings in the Hydesville, New York, home of the Fox family, during March 1848, reached France in 1850. According to French philosopher and historian Ernest Bersot, it quickly became a passion. People sat around tables for hours in anxious expectation of hearing from the spirits. During the winter, there was no other social occupation or topic. The Catholic Church condemned it, but few paid attention.

As mass communication in those years was extremely limited, it seems incredible that the "epidemic" could have spread so far, so rapidly. This seems to give credence to the spirit messages recorded by Professor Robert Hare, as discussed in Chapter One, that a delegation of advanced spirits was behind it and Hydesville was simply a launching point.

Intrigued by the interest in spirit communication, French educator and author Hippolyte Léon Dénizarth Rivail, who later adopted the pseudonym Allan Kardec (hereinafter, "Kardec"), began a careful investigation. Born in Lyons to a distinguished family, Kardec was educated at the Institute of Pestalozzi at Yverdum. He had intended to enter the legal profession, as had his father and grandfather, but, in 1828, he purchased a school for boys and devoted himself to education. In 1830, at age twenty-five, he began giving free lectures to the public on chemistry, physics, comparative anatomy, and astronomy. Under his given name, he authored a number of books aimed at improving education in the public schools of France.

Although the exact year is uncertain, Kardec's introduction to mediumship apparently came in 1854 at the home of a friend, Emile Charles Baudin, whose daughters, Caroline, sixteen, and Julie, thirteen, were mediums. Most of the communication coming through the two teenagers was frivolous or mundane, but when Kardec was present the messages became serious and profound. When Kardec inquired as to the cause of the change in disposition, he was informed that "spirits of a much higher order than those who habitually communicated through the two young mediums came expressly for him, and would continue to do so, in order to enable him to fulfill an important religious mission" (Kardec 1857).

It was these advanced spirits who told him to adopt the Allan Kardec pseudonym for the books he would write "in the fulfillment of the mission which, as we have already told you, has been confided to you by Providence, and which will gradually open before you as you proceed in it under our guidance" (Kardec 1857).

Kardec would meet with the one or both of the mediums a couple of evenings every week and put questions to the spirits. He approached his investigation scientifically, searching for mechanistic explanations. The earliest manifestations of intelligence were made by table tipping, with the legs of table moving up and down a given number of times to reply "yes" or "no" to questions asked. "Even here, it must be confessed," Kardec wrote in his 1857 book, *Le Livre des Esprits (The Spirits' Book)*, "there was nothing very convincing for the incredulous, as these apparent answers might be an effect

Allan Kardec.

of chance. But fuller answers were soon obtained, the table striking a number of blows corresponding to the number of each letter of the alphabet, so that words and sentences began to be produced in reply to questions propounded" (Kardec 1857).

As this method of communication was slow and inconvenient, the communicating agent suggested that Kardec fit a pencil to a small basket (a planchette) and place it on a sheet of paper. The basket "was then set in motion by the same occult power that moved the tables; but instead of obeying a simple and regular movement of rotation, the pencil traced letters that formed words, sentences, and entire discourses, filling many pages, treating of the deepest questions of philosophy, morality, metaphysics, psychology, etc., and as rapidly as though written by hand" (Kardec 1857). Kardec explained that the medium would merely lay her fingers on the edges of the planchette in such a way that it would be impossible for her to guide it in any direction whatever. A further observation lending credibility to the process had to do with the fact that the handwriting changed completely with each spirit who communicated and that when a spirit reappeared the same writing resumed.

As the planchette writing was also slow, further experimentation by Kardec resulted in a change to trance mediumship, in which answers were orally transmitted, and automatic writing, in which the medium held a pencil and "was made to write under an impulsion independent of his will, and often with an almost feverish rapidity" (Kardec 1857). There was no doubt in Kardec's mind that the nature of the communication was far beyond the comprehension of the young sisters. "The replies thus given, and the messages thus transmitted, are sometimes marked by such sagacity, profundity, and appropriateness, and convey thoughts so elevated, so sublime, that they can only emanate from a superior intelligence imbued with the purest morality," Kardec wrote, going on to mention that at other times the communication was so frivolous and trivial that it could not have come from the same source (Kardec 1857). It became clear to Kardec that both "higher spirits"

Automatic writing.

and "foolish and lying spirits" were communicating through the mediums. He likened it to a dinner party in which the discussion might have to do with the nature of the soul or death. While some members at the table might take the discussion very seriously, others, perhaps the materialists, would treat it cynically and sarcastically.

Kardec pointed out that even the higher spirits would tell him that they do not have all the answers, that there is disagreement among them, and that we should not accept everything said by them as literal truth. While these higher spirits may be more advanced than we are, they have not yet achieved perfection and are not all-knowing, Kardec was informed. They are attempting to assist us to the best of their ability, but they are certainly not infallible. Further, Kardec was told that human languages are too limited when it comes to describing spirit matters. "…even spirits who are really enlightened may express themselves in terms which appear to be different, but which, at bottom, mean the same thing, especially in regard to matters which your language is incapable of expressing clearly, and which can only be spoken to you by means of figures and comparisons that you mistake for literal statements of fact," was an explanation recorded by Kardec (Kardec 1857).

When Kardec asked a question about the nature of God, the reply came: "God exists. You cannot doubt His existence, and that is the one essential point. Do not seek to go beyond it; do not lose yourself in the labyrinth which, for you, is without an issue. Such inquiries would not make you better; they would rather tend to add to your pride, by causing you to imagine that you knew something, while, in reality, you would know nothing…Study your own imperfections, that you may get rid of them; this will be far more useful to you than the vain attempt to penetrate the impenetrable" (Kardec 1857).

Kardec labeled the philosophy given to him by the spirits "spiritism" rather than spiritualism, explaining that spiritualism, used in its broadest sense, is the opposite of materialism, and anyone who believes in something more than matter is a spiritualist. That would include members of ortho-dox religions who are opposed to spirit communication. Moreover, organized groups were forming in both the United States and Great Britain and calling themselves spiritualists, thereby narrowing the term. These groups, while agreeing on most things, were in conflict on some issues, especially on the role of Christ and on reincarnation. The spirits communicating with Kardec embraced both Christ and reincarnation.

When Kardec asked the spirits in what sense we should understand the words of Christ, "My kingdom is not of this world," the response came: "Christ, in replying thus, spoke figuratively. He meant to say that He reigned only over pure and unselfish hearts. He is wherever the love of goodness holds sway; but they who are greedy for things of this world, and attached to the enjoyments of earth, are not with Him" (Kardec 1857).

When Kardec asked about the aim of reincarnation, the reply was: "It is a necessity upon [spirits] by God, as the means of attaining perfection. For some of them it is an expiation; for others a mission. In order to attain perfection, it is necessary for them to undergo all the vicissitudes of corporeal existence. It is the experience acquired by expiation that constitutes its usefulness. Incarnation has also another aim—viz. that of fitting the spirit to perform his share in the work of creation…" (Kardec 1857).

Even during those early days of mediumship, explanations other than fraud or spirit agency were being advanced by scholars and scientists. They weren't called "telepathy" and "super-ESP," as they are now, but the concept was the same. As for the theory that the information coming from the medium was emanating from her subconscious or that the medium was tapping into the minds of the sitters around her (i.e., telepathy), Kardec wondered how this theory might explain information or communication entirely foreign to the thoughts, knowledge, or opinions of the medium or those present, as he had so often observed.

The "radiation of thought" theory, what is now called super-ESP (or superpsi) held that the ability of the medium to access information goes well beyond those around her, extending to any part of the globe, while according to the "universal radiation" theory there is some kind of universal memory (a computer in the ethers?) which the medium can tap into and access any information. Although unable to disprove them, Kardec asked why such theories, seemingly more marvelous than the spirit agency theory, were easier for some to accept. Clearly, such explanations were non-materialistic in nature, suggesting some kind of "Higher Power" at work. In effect, these theories suggested a God without an afterlife, or at least without spirits. "It is possible to be very clever, very learned, and yet to lack clearness of judgment," Kardec summed up his thoughts on these alternate theories (Kardec 1857).

A year or so before Kardec began his investigation, a renowned fellow Frenchman, author Victor Hugo, was introduced to table-tapping. Shortly after arriving, as a political exile, on the island of Jersey in the English Channel on August 5, 1853, Hugo and his family were entertaining Delphine de Girardin, a journalist and a childhood friend, at their home. After dinner, de Girardin suggested they experiment with some tabletipping. Highly skeptical, Hugo declined. However, his wife, Adéle, agreed to it. Nothing happened that first night. They tried again the next night, but still without results.

It took another five or six nights of patiently sitting around a table before it began tapping out words, and then only after Hugo, his son Charles, and several others joined the two women. When Hugo asked for an identity, the table tapped out, "d-e-a-d g-i-r-l." When he asked for a name, the table tapped out, "l-e-o-p-o-l-d-i-n-e." Léopoldine was Hugo's beloved daughter, who had drowned twelve years earlier at age nineteen. Further questioning followed in which short answers were provided. However, Hugo remained skeptical, suggesting that the sitters somehow made the table act through their thoughts. If it were indeed a spirit, Hugo wondered how he could know for sure it was his daughter and not some impostor spirit posing as her. After a number of other sittings, he apparently came to believe that it was his daughter's spirit communicating.

What may have convinced Hugo was communication on December 9, 1853, from André Chénier, a French poet, who was executed at the guillotine on July 25, 1794. He tapped out the remainder of the poem he had been working on just before his execution. It was in the same style as his work when living. He also produced new poems in the highest literary style, joining together a number of the poems he wrote when alive.

Chénier told of his last moments on earth, seeing the slop basket swaying beneath his head, half-filled with blood from those executed before him, and, suddenly, hearing the odd creaking sound above his head. After the sensation that his head was falling into the slop basket, he found himself far above his headless body, his soul body being enveloped in a diaphanous sheath. He then felt the presence of his mother and mistress. He observed a luminous line separating his head from his body as his head rolled into the gutter and his body was dragged away.

During February 1854, the Jersey circle made contact with a spirit identifying himself as Martin Luther, the father of Protestantism. Hugo asked Luther why God does not better reveal himself, to which Luther replied: "Because doubt is the instrument which forges the human spirit. If the day were to come when the human spirit no longer doubted, the human soul would fly off and leave the plough behind, for it would have acquired wings. The earth would lie fallow. Now, God is the sower and man the harvester. The celestial seed demands that the human ploughshare remain in the furrow of life" (Chambers 1998).

Still, Hugo continued to ask other spirits the same question, finally deciding that he wasn't going to ask again. "It's becoming obvious to me," he wrote, "from what the table said this evening—and on several other occasions as well—that this world of the sublime, which has consented to communicate with our world of shadows, will not allow itself to be forced by us to reveal its secrets…The world of the sublime wants to remain sublime" (Chambers 1998).

The Teachings of Spiritism

The Spirits' Book, first published by Allan Kardec in 1857, contains 1,019 questions and answers concerning the spirit world. Kardec would put questions to the higher spirits and then record the answers. Reproductions of this book are still available through Internet sources. Here is a sampling of what the spirits told Kardec (the number at the end of each indicates the number of the question in the book):

God: "Poverty of human speech [is] incompetent to define what transcends human intelligence"(3).

Infinity in space: "Suppose the existence of boundaries, what would there be beyond them? This consideration confounds human reason; and nevertheless your reason itself tells you that it cannot be otherwise. It is thus with the idea of infinity, under whatever aspect you consider it. The idea of infinity cannot be comprehended in your narrow space" (35).

Alien life: "There are many men having a high opinion of themselves who even imagine that your little globe alone, of all the countless myriads of globes around you, has the privilege of being inhabited by reasoning beings. They fancy that God has created the universe for them alone. Insensate vanity!" (55).

Creation of spirits: "If spirits had not had a beginning, they would be equal with God; whereas they are His creation, and subject to His will. That God has existed from all eternity is incontestable; but as to when and how He created us, we know nothing. You may say that we have had no beginning in this sense, that God being eternal, He must have incessantly created. But as to when and how each of us was made, this, I repeat, is known to no one. It is the great mystery" (78).

Spirits defined: "How is it possible to define a thing in regard to which no terms of comparison exist, and which your language is incompetent to express? Can one who is born blind define light? 'Immaterial' is not the right word; 'incorporeal' would be nearer the truth, something real. Spirit is quintessentialised matter, but matter existing in a state which has no analogue within the circle of your comprehension, and so ethereal that it could not be perceived by your senses" (82).

Awakening after death: "This depends entirely on their degree of elevation. He who has already accomplished a certain amount of purification recovers his consciousness almost immediately, because he had already freed himself from the thralldom of materiality during his bodily life; whereas the carnally minded man, he whose conscience is not clear, retains the impression of matter for a much longer time" (164)..

Attending one's own funeral: "Spirits very often do so; but, in many cases, without understanding what is going on, being still in the state of confusion that usually follows death" (327).

Location of spirits: "Spirits are everywhere; the infinitudes of space are peopled with them in infinite numbers. Unperceived by you, they are incessantly beside you, observing and acting upon you; for spirits are one of the powers of Nature, and are the instruments employed by God for the accomplishment of His providential designs. But all spirits do not go everywhere; there are regions of which the entrance is interdicted to those who are less advanced" (87).

Spirit appearance: "Not for eyes such as yours; but, for us, they have a form, though one only to be vaguely imagined by you as a flame, a gleam, or an ethereal spark. If you could see it, it would appear to you to vary from a dull gray to the brilliancy of the ruby, according to the degree of the spirit's purity" (88).

Spirit travel: "A spirit can travel in either way (cognizant or not of distance). He can, if he will, take cognizance of the distance he passes through, or he can rid himself entirely of the sense of distance. This depends on the spirit's will, and also on his degree of purity" (90).

Equality of spirits: "They are of different degrees according to the degree of purification to which they have attained" (96).

On seeing God: "Only spirits of the highest order see and understand Him; spirits of lower order feel and divine Him" (244).

High spirits: "They unite, in a very high degree, scientific knowledge, wisdom, and goodness. Their language, inspired only by the purest benevolence, is always noble and elevated, often sublime. Their superiority renders them more apt than any others to impart to us just and true ideas in relation to the incorporeal world, within the limits of the knowledge permitted to mankind. They willingly enter into communication with those who seek truth in simplicity and sincerity, and who are sufficiently freed from the bonds of materiality to be capable of understanding it" (111).

Low-level spirits: "Some of them are inactive and neutral, not doing either good or evil; others, on the contrary, take pleasure in evil, and are delighted when they find an opportunity of doing wrong. Others, again, are frivolous, foolish, fantastic, mischievous rather than wicked, tricksy rather than positively malicious; amusing themselves by mystifying the human beings on whom they are able to act, and causing them various petty annoyances for their own diversion" (99).

Education of low-level spirits: "They study their past, and seek out the means of raising themselves to a higher degree. Possessed of vision, they observe all that is going on in the regions through which they pass. They listen to the discourse of enlightened men, and to the counsels of spirits more advanced than themselves, and they thus acquire new ideas" (227).

Happiness of low-level spirits: "More or less so according to their deserts. They suffer from the passions of which they have retained the principle, or they are happy in proportion as they are more or less dematerialized. In the state of erraticity, a spirit perceives what he needs in order to become happier, and he is thus stimulated to seek out the means of attaining what he lacks. But he is not always permitted to reincarnate himself when he desires to do so, and the prolongation of erraticity then becomes a punishment" (231).

What spirits see concerning humans: "They can [see everything] if they choose, since they are incessantly around you. But, practically, each spirit sees only those things to which he directs his attention; for he pays no heed to those which do not interest him" (456).

Spirit influence: "Their influence upon [your thoughts and actions] is greater than you suppose, for it is very often they who direct both" (459).

Negative spirit influence: "Imperfect spirits are used by Providence as instruments for trying men's faith and constancy in well-doing. You, being a spirit, must advance in the knowledge of the infinite. It is for this end that you are made to pass through the trials of evil in order to attain goodness. Our mission is to lead you into the right road. When you are acted upon by evil influence, it is because you attract evil spirits to you by your evil desires, for evil spirits always come to aid you in doing the evil you desire to do; they can only help you to do wrong when you give way to evil desires. If you are inclined to commit murder, you will have about you a swarm of spirits who will keep this inclination alive in you; but you will also have others about you who will try to influence you for good, which restores the balance, and leaves you of your decision" (466).

Spirits seeing the future: "That again, depends on their degree of advancement. Very often, they foresee it only partially; but, even when they foresee it more clearly, they are not always permitted to reveal it. When they foresee it, it appears to them to be present. A spirit sees the future more clearly in proportion as he approaches God. After death, the soul sees and embraces at a glance all its past emigrations, but it cannot see what God has in store for it" (243).

Heaven and Hell: "They are only symbols; there are happy and unhappy spirits everywhere. Nevertheless, as we have also told you, spirits of the same order are brought together by sympathy; but, when they are perfect, they can meet together wherever they will" (1012).

Eternal suffering: "God has not created beings to let them remain for ever a prey to evil; He created them only in a state of simplicity and ignorance, and all of them must progress, in a longer or shorter time, according to the action of their will" (1006).

Three

Sir William Crookes Validates D. D. Home

I never said it was possible, I only said it was true.

—Sir William Crookes

On December 16, 1868, three young men stared out the window of a third-floor room in a London mansion and could not believe what they were seeing—another man floating in the air. He was Daniel Dunglas Home, a 35-year-old Scottish-American medium.

The three witnesses were Lord Lindsay, Lord Adare, and Captain Charles Wynne. They had gathered at Lindsay's home to take part in a séance by Home (pronounced "Hoom"). After the three men and Home were seated, Home slumped in his chair and went into a trance. He then got up and walked out of the room. The three men apparently didn't know what to make of the departure and remained seated. They then heard the sound of a window in the adjoining room being raised. They looked out the window in their room and saw Home standing on air, three stories above the ground. Home then floated to the closed window out of which they were looking, opened it, stepped into the room, went to his chair, and sat down, still in a trance state. As the three men questioned what they had seen and wondered how Home got out the window in the adjoining room, which was open only a foot or so, Home got up from his chair, walked to the other room, went through the open space, head first, and then floated back in the same window, feet first.

Most who heard the story suggested that Home was a hypnotist or a magician, or that the four men had had too much to drink. However, Sir William Crookes, one of England's most distinguished scientists, began investigating spiritual phenomena two years later, in 1870, and also observed Home being levitated. "The most striking cases of levitation which I have witnessed have been with Mr. Home," Crookes wrote, stating that he saw Home levitated on three different occasions and that there were at least a hundred recorded instances of Home rising from the ground in the presence of many credible witnesses (Crookes 1922).

"To reject the recorded evidence on this subject is to reject all human testimony whatever; for no fact in sacred or profane history is supported by a stronger array of proofs," added Crookes, who took every possible precaution to rule out fraud (Crookes 1922).

As Crookes came to understand it, Home did not levitate on his own. He *was levitated* by his spirit controls. Besides Home and heavy furniture, the spirits levitated other people, played musical instruments without touching them, and produced luminous hands that would float in front of those present, touch them, and hand them objects. The "dead" also spoke through Home.

Crookes, a Fellow of the Royal Society, studied and taught at the Royal College of Chemistry before becoming a meteorologist at the Radcliffe Observatory, Oxford. In 1858, he inherited enough money to set up his own laboratory in London, In 1861, he discovered the element thallium, and later invented the radiometer, the spinthariscope, and the Crookes tube, a high-vacuum tube which contributed to the discovery of the X-ray. He was founder and editor of *Chemical News* and later served as editor of the *Quarterly Journal of Science*. Knighted in 1897 for his scientific work, he was not someone to be easily duped or to fabricate strange stories. In fact, Crookes undertook

D. D. Home.

D. D. Home levitating.

Sir William Crookes.

psychical research with the intent of demonstrating that the alleged phenomena of spiritualism were all fraudulent. He opined that the increased employment of scientific methods would drive the "worthless residuum of spiritualism" into the unknown limbo of magic and necromancy.

Crookes was not the first person in England to investigate mediums. Professor Augustus De Morgan, chairman of the mathematics department at the University College in London and a reformer in mathematical logic, began sitting with mediums in 1853. "I have seen in my house frequently, various persons presenting themselves [as mediums]," De Morgan wrote in his memoirs. "The answers are given mostly by the table, on which a hand or two is gently placed, tilting up at the letters…I have no theory about it, but in a year or two something may turn up. I am, however, satisfied of the reality of the phenomenon. A great many other persons are as cognizant of these phenomena in their own houses as myself. Make what you can of it if you are a philosopher" (Doyle 1926).

Alfred Russel Wallace, co-originator with Charles Darwin of the natural selection theory of evolution, also had a number of sittings with mediums beginning in 1865 and satisfied himself that much of the phenomena he witnessed were real. Wallace said that he was a confirmed philosophical skeptic and so thorough a materialist that he simply refused to accept the conception of spiritual existence before he began his sittings with a Mrs. Marshall of London. He later stated that he felt that the evidence for the genuineness of mediumship was as strong as it was for any other branch of science. In 1869, the Dialectical Society of London appointed a committee, including Wallace, to investigate mediumship. The committee returned a report that genuine phenomena exist, a decision not well received by the society. It is believed to have been that report that prompted Crookes to begin investigating mediums.

Crookes had his first sitting with Home on April 21, 1870. Except for raps and strong movements of the table, Crookes and his small circle of friends did not experience anything worth mentioning. Sittings on May 17

Alfred Russel Wallace.

and June 3 were likewise without significant phenomena. On July 8, raps were again heard and by calling out the alphabet and asking for a name, they got the letters "P-H-I-L" (possibly Philip Crookes, William's brother, who had died three years earlier). Invisible hands were felt by all six sitters and Crookes's handkerchief was pulled away from him and carried to his brother Walter's hand on the other end of the table. However, there was no significant communication with "Phil."

On July 19, 1870, Crookes recorded that an invisible hand—one that felt solid to the sitters—took Mrs. Wiseman's handkerchief, carried it in front of him, and then returned it to Mrs. Wiseman. Crookes stated that he definitely saw an appearance of fingers. He felt something placed in his hand by the invisible hand and discovered it was a bell which had been on the other side of the table. Home held an accordion between the thumb and middle finger of one hand, hanging it vertically, with his other hand clearly on the table for all to see. Yet, a simple tune came from it. By a prearranged code, five notes were sounded, indicating that the spirit wanted to communicate. The letters of the alphabet were spelled out and the message was: "This is unscientific science." The German song "Fatherland" was then played "in a very beautiful manner." Crookes asked if the spirit who was supposedly playing it knew how to play the accordion when alive. The spirit replied that he did not, although he had a taste for music. Several other spirits communicated that night, but Crookes did not keep thorough records of the communication, admitting many years later that he did not give enough attention to recording the communication as he was more interested in observing the physical side of the phenomena.

The séance on April 12, 1871, Crookes recorded, was the most exciting and satisfactory he experienced, probably because two other mediums were present and added to Home's psychic force. At first, they had very rough manifestations, chairs knocking about, a table floating above the floor and then being slammed down, loud and unpleasant noises, what Crookes termed "phenomena of a low class." It was well known by this time that harmony among the sitters was necessary for good results and this harmony could often be achieved by singing. Thus, they began singing in hopes of improving conditions. After the group song, Home sung solo, what Crookes referred to as "a sacred piece," after which one of the other mediums "was carried right up, floated across the table and dropped with a crash of pictures and ornaments at the other end of the room" (Medhurst 1972). When Home sang again, both of the other mediums were lifted up by the invisible spirits and placed on the table. Crookes surmised that the other two mediums brought low-class influences with them and Home's singing drove them away, allowing his good ones to enter.

They then sang, "For he's a jolly good fellow," after which they heard a "very sweet voice" high over their heads say, "You should rather give praise to God." They tried a more sacred song, after which Home's accordion was lifted up from the table and floated about the room, sometimes going well outside the circle in which all, including Home, were holding hands. It played what Crookes called one of the most exquisite sacred pieces he had ever heard, as a "fine male spirit" voice accompanied it. Crookes noted that the movement of the instrument was very rapid and often seemed to be in two places at once. It stopped right in front of him and others as it played with no visible hands. Voices then came and addressed them, but Crookes did not record what they spoke about.

While the group continued to sit, each holding the hand of the person next to him or her, Serjeant Cox, a lawyer who frequented many of the sittings, had a book taken from his pocket. He liberated his hand long enough to catch the invisible hand removing the book. However, it eluded his grasp and the book floated across the table and was gently laid in front of Mrs. Crookes. Then hands came to nearly all of them as their faces were stroked and hands patted. Cox's gloves were floated around the room as was Home's handkerchief. Crookes wrote that it was impossible to describe all the striking things that took place that night or to convey the intense feeling of genuineness and reality.

All of that took place in Crookes's seventh sitting with Home. Over the next two years, he would have another twenty-one sittings with the medium. They would take place at Crookes's home or at the home of other sitters, never at Home's place of residence. Even though Crookes soon became convinced of Home's honesty and integrity, he continued to take strict precautions in order to rule out some sort of conjuring by Home. When the table was levitating, he would check Home's legs and feet to be sure that they were not somehow involved in lifting the heavy table. On several occasions, he also measured the foot pounds of pressure on the table as it levitated. Unlike many mediums, Home did not insist upon darkness and so there was no problem in observing him while the phenomena was taking place. Crookes even purchased an accordion to rule out the possibility of Home's accordion having some special parts to it. Crookes's accordion performed just as Home's did, floating around the room while giving out music.

There were times when the phenomena were very limited or when Home felt that there was too much negativity for good results. One such case was when a sitter was absolutely certain that Home was a charlatan. Another was on Derby Day in London. Home said the moral atmosphere was so negatively charged from all the gambling and drunkenness that nothing would come through, even after some music.

Many affluent and distinguished people were among the sitters, including Dr. Wallace. On one occasion, Wallace and Crookes, two of the world's most famous scientists, were crawling around under a levitating table searching for some kind of physical explanation. Wallace defended Crookes and Home against attacks by other scientists who had concluded that Home was a magician. One of them, Sir David Brewster, sat with Home and saw a table levitate right in front of him, but still concluded that since there was no natural explanation for what he saw that Home had to be a magician. Brewster scoffed at the idea that spirits played a part in it and saw no other explanation beyond sleight of hand that was beyond his understanding.

But why so much tomfoolery—handkerchiefs being removed from

pockets, floating accordions, people being lifted and dropped in another part of the room? One would think that spirits would have a little more class. Were these simply mischievous earthbound spirits? On June 28, 1871, in Crookes's eighteenth sitting with Home, some answers concerning this were given. While Home was in an entranced state, a voice came through him. One of the sitters asked who was speaking. "It is not one spirit in particular," the response came. "It is a general influence. It requires two or three spirits to get complete control over Dan. The conditions are not very good tonight." The communicating "entity" explained that there were very few spirits able to communicate and that they were experimenting on their side just as Crookes and the others were on their side. "Sometimes they think they have found out some of the conditions which will lead to success, and the next time something occurs which shows them they know scarcely anything about it," the voice coming through Home said (Medhurst 1972).

It had been explained to Professor Robert Hare, some twenty years earlier (see Chapter One), that the physical phenomena were simply to offer proof of the existence of the spirit world and to draw attention to the communications.

The phenomena continued through Crookes's last sitting on May 28, 1873—floating objects, luminous hands, strange luminous vapors, beautiful music from an accordion with no hands on it, voices talking and singing, levitations. In one of the levitations in front of the circle, Crookes reported that Home rose about eighteen inches off the ground, and he (Crookes) passed his hands under his feet and over his head. On another occasion, Home was levitated while sitting in his chair. In still another sitting, Ellen Crookes, William's wife, was levitated while in her chair.

In his autobiography, *Incidents in My Life*, published in 1862, well before Crookes was introduced to him, Home wrote that during his elevations, or levitations, that he experienced an electrical fullness about his feet. He was usually lifted up perpendicularly with his arms rigid and drawn above his head, as if he were grasping the unseen power raising him from the floor. At times, he would reach the ceiling and then be moved into a reclining position. Some of the levitations lasted four or five minutes.

Born in Scotland on March 20, 1833, Home moved to the United States with an uncle and aunt when he was nine, growing up in Troy, New York, and Norwich, Connecticut. His mother, he wrote, had the gift of "second sight." He recalled that when he was seventeen and living in Norwich and his mother was living in Waterford, twelve miles away, he got an impression that she wanted to see him. He walked to her home and she told him that she would be leaving him (dying) in four months. She explained that her deceased daughter, Mary, came to her in a vision and broke the news to her. Four months later, the prophecy was fulfilled as Home's mother became ill and passed into spirit. That night, before word reached him, Home's mother appeared to him and told him she had departed. However, Home's first clairvoyant experience came at age thirteen, when a boyhood friend from Troy, three hundred miles away, came to him to tell him he had died three days earlier.

Several months after his mother's death in 1850, loud raps began in the home of the aunt and uncle who had adopted Home. Home recalled that his aunt immediately attributed the disturbances to him and concluded it was the devil's work. One evening, the table and chairs began moving around on their own. His aunt threw herself on a moving table and was lifted up with it from the floor. While visiting another aunt in the area, the same phenomena occurred. This aunt was more understanding, and having heard about the Fox sisters of Hydesville and how communication was effected by so many raps being given for each letter of the alphabet, she began to ask questions and get intelligent replies. Home's mother communicated: "Daniel, fear not, my child, God is with you, and who shall be against you? Seek to do good: be truthful and truth-loving, and you will prosper my child. Yours is a glorious mission—you will convince the infidel, cure the sick, and console the weeping" (Home 1862). From that point on, Home's mediumship developed rapidly. Not only did he find himself communing with spirits, he soon realized that he had the gift of healing. His reputation spread and in 1855, he traveled to England, where poet Elizabeth Barrett Browning became one of his most ardent supporters, although her husband, poet Robert Browning, a dogmatic disbeliever in psychic phenomena, took a dislike to Home and labeled him "Mr. Sludge, the Medium." But Home was called upon to give demonstrations of his gifts to royalty and aristocracy throughout Europe. In 1856, Home became a Catholic, but eight years later the Church excommunicated him as a "sorcerer." He died in 1886 at age fifty-three.

There is evidence indicating the Home's mediumship played a significant role in converting Professor Robert Hare and the Rev. William Stainton Moses to a belief in mediumship.

"Of all the persons endowed with a powerful development of this Psychic Force, and who have been termed 'mediums' upon quite another theory of its origin, Mr. Daniel Dunglas Home is the most remarkable," Crookes wrote, "and it is mainly owing to the many opportunities I have had of carrying on my investigations in his presence that I am enabled to affirm so conclusively the existence of this Force" (Crookes 1922).

Shortly after completing his investigation of Home, Crookes began investigating the mediumship of Florence Cook, who purportedly was able to produce a full human form materialization of a spirit named "Katie King." In 1874, Crookes called Cook's mediumship genuine, stating that he had not only witnessed the materialization of Katie King but touched her, talked with her, and photographed her.

The scientific community was shocked by Crookes's endorsement of Home and Cook. As a result, he came under attack by many closed-minded scientists—those who shared Sir David Brewster's attitude that such phenomena were completely opposed to scientific law and therefore there was no explanation other than that Crookes had been duped. Various theories were offered as to how he had been deceived. It mattered not that Wallace had observed Home's ability as had a number of other scholars and scientists, nor that Dr. Charles Richet, an esteemed French physicist and winner of the 1913 Nobel Prize in medicine, also witnessed Katie King materializations and, like Crookes, concluded that they were genuine.

Apparently wearied by the attacks, Crookes gave up psychical research and returned to orthodox science. While he maintained a private interest in psychical research, he spoke very little of the subject in public, often very guarded and occasionally indicating that the "psychic force" he had witnessed may not have been the work of spirits. However, in a speech before the *British Association for the Advancement of Science* in 1898, he said he had nothing to retract. His writings in subsequent years indicate that he returned to a belief in spirits and, concomitantly, the survival of consciousness at death. In fact, in 1917, a year or so after his wife's death, Crookes is said to have had a lively conversation with her at a London séance. He died in 1919 at age eighty-six. Whether he ever again met up with Home has not been recorded.

One of the scientists who lambasted Crookes for not debunking Home and Cook was Dr. Julian Ochorowicz, professor of psychology and philosophy at the University of Warsaw and one of the founders of the Polish Psychological Institute in Warsaw. After he began investigating psychical phenomena, he changed his views. "I found I had done a great wrong to men who had proclaimed new truths at the risk of their positions," he confessed. "When I remember that I branded as a fool that fearless investigator, Crookes, the inventor of the radiometer, because he had the courage to assert the reality of psychic phenomena and to subject them to scientific tests, and when I also recollect that I used to read his articles thereon in the same stupid style, regarding him as crazy, I am ashamed, both of myself and others, and I cry from the very bottom of my heart. 'Father, I have sinned against the Light'" (Tweedale 1925).

Four

Moses, Imperator, and the Spiritual Band of Forty-Nine

With the even tenor of this straightforward and reputable life [of W. Stainton Moses] was inwoven a chain of mysteries which, in whatever way they be explained, make that life one of the most extraordinary which our century has seen.

—Frederic W. H. Myers

Like so many other members of the clergy, the Rev. William Stainton Moses, a minister of the Church of England, frowned upon spiritualism—spirit communication through mediums—considering it all trickery and fraud. He called Lord Adare's book on Daniel Dunglas Home, the Scottish-American physical medium, the "dreariest twaddle" he had ever come across.

Having received his master's degree from Oxford, Moses began his ministry in the Isle of Man in 1863. He faithfully served the Anglican Church until 1869, when he became seriously ill and was forced to resign his curacy. Following a convalescent period, he was appointed English Master in University College, London, a position he would hold until 1889. It was during the early part of his convalescence that his views on spiritualism began to change. He had befriended Dr. and Mrs. Stanhope Templeman Speer and became a tutor to their son, Charlton Templeman Speer. In Moses's biography, penned many years later, Charlton explained that Moses and his father frequently discussed religious matters and both were gradually drifting into an unorthodox, almost agnostic, frame of mind. Mrs. Speer had taken an interest in spiritualism and persuaded her husband and Moses to attend a séance with Miss Lottie Fowler. During that sitting, on April 2, 1872, Moses received some very evidential information about a friend who had died. His curiosity aroused, Moses attended other séances, including some with Home. Dr. Speer, who had earlier called it all "stuff and nonsense," shared his friend's curiosity and joined in.

After a few months, Moses was convinced that he was indeed communicating with the spirit world, and soon thereafter he began to realize that he was a medium himself. According to Charlton Speer, a small circle of friends gathered regularly to observe and record the phenomena. They included himself, Dr. and Mrs. Speer, a Dr. Thompson, Serjeant Cox, and several others. Occasionally, Professor William Crookes (later Sir William), the distinguished chemist and psychical researcher, would attend the circle. As reported by Cox (Myers 1961), a lawyer, Moses (or the spirits controlling him) could, by simply placing his hands on it, levitate a large mahogany table which otherwise required the strength of two men to move it an inch. The spirits levitated Moses at least three times, on one occasion raising him on the table and then lifting him from the table to an adjacent sofa.

Apports were frequently seen by the sitters—objects coming mysteriously through closed doors or walls and thrown upon the table from a direction mostly over Moses's head. Some of the objects came from various rooms in the house, but the origin of others, including ivory crosses, corals, pearls, and precious stones, was unknown. Psychic lights were frequently observed, usually when Moses was in trance. They would pass through solid objects. Unusual scents, most often musk, were produced, and a wide variety of music sounds were heard, even though there were no musical instruments

William Stainton Moses.

in the room. The sitters also observed luminous hands and columns of light vaguely suggesting human forms. These phenomena were apparently produced only to convince Moses and the sitters of the supernormal powers of the communicators.

Charlton Speer recalled a time when they were sitting as usual in the study of his parents' home. He had in front of him some blank note paper and a pencil. Moses told Charlton that he saw a very bright column of light behind him and that it had developed into a spirit form. Charlton asked him if the face was familiar and Moses replied in the negative. When the séance was concluded, Charlton discovered a message and a signature on his notepad. As a musician himself, Charlton recognized the name as that of a distinguished musician who had died during the early part of the century. Without telling Moses the name of the musician, he brought out several albums containing photographs of various celebrities and asked Moses if he could pick out the spirit he had seen. Sure enough, he picked the composer who had delivered the message to Charlton.

Communication with spirits began, according to Charlton Speer, with a variety of raps and progressed to the direct voice, direct writing, the trance voice, and automatic writing. The direct voice, in which voices came through in the air above them, was not clear or distinct, while direct writing, in which a pencil untouched by human hands gave short messages, such as that received from the distinguished musician, was rare. Speer reported that the trance voice, in which the spirits used Moses's entranced body, came through in a dignified, temperate, clear and convincing tone. Moreover, it was always apparent that the personality addressing the group was not that of the medium. The voices were different and the ideas expressed were often contrary to Moses's. While different spirits came through, the chief communicator called himself Imperator. Mrs. Speer did the recording of the trance messages, but she said it was impossible for her to capture the beauty and refinement of the manifestations or the power and dignity of Imperator's influence.

"I, myself, Imperator Servus Dei, am the chief of a band of forty-nine spirits, the presiding and controlling spirit, under whose guidance and direction the others work," Mrs. Speer recorded. "I come from the seventh sphere to work out the will of the Almighty; and, when my work is complete, I shall return to those spheres of bliss from which none returns again to earth. But this will not be till the medium's work on earth is finished, and his mission on earth exchanged for a wider one in the spheres" (*Meilach.com*). Imperator added that spirits named Rector and Doctor were his immediate assistants. He had come, he said, to explain the spirit world, how it is controlled, and the way in which information is conveyed to humans. "Man must judge according to the light of reason that is in him." Imperator voiced through Moses. "That is the ultimate standard, and the progressive soul will receive what the ignorant or prejudiced will reject. God's truth is forced on none" (Moses 1924).

When Imperator was speaking through Moses, the sitters observed a large, bright cross of light behind Moses's head and rays surrounding it. The lights seemed to culminate in a beautiful line of light of great brilliancy several feet high and moving from side to side. One of the sitters asked Imperator to explain the lights. He responded that the pillar of light was himself, the bright light behind him was his attendants, and the numerous lights seen in the room belonged to the band of forty-nine. In all, there were seven circles of seven spirits each. Each circle comprised one presiding spirit with a particular mission and six ministers. One of the forty-nine, a spirit calling himself Elliotson, said that it was their desire to show that God Himself is the center of influence and that His influence flows through intermediary agencies, permeating humanity. This angelic influence diffuses itself around those it is able to reach. Man becomes the means of disseminating the knowledge of which he is the unconscious recipient.

When Dr. Speer asked about the teachings of orthodox religion, Imperator responded that while the Bible was intended as the very word of God in both matter and form, much of what has been recorded and accepted as truth is a result of improper filtering and interpretation. "Nay, the communicating spirits are perforce obliged to use the material which is found in the medium's mind, moulding and fashioning it for their purposes: erasing fallacies, inspiring new views of truth, but working on the material which is already gathered," Imperator explained. "The purity of the spirit message depends much on the passivity of the medium and on the conditions under which the message is communicated. Hence, in your Bible there are traces here and there of the individuality of the medium; of errors caused by imperfect control; of the colour of his opinions; as well as of special peculiarities addressed to the special needs of the people to whom the message was first given, and for whose case it was primarily adapted" (Moses 1924).

Imperator went on to say that those in the spirit world often attempt to convey spiritual concepts which are inconceivable to those in the flesh and in doing this they sometimes misuse human expressions. Much of what they communicate, he said, is thus necessarily allegorical. "You must not insist too strongly on literal meanings of words used by us to describe what exists only with us, which finds no counterpart in your world, and transcends your present knowledge, and which therefore can only be approximately described in language borrowed from earth," Imperator continued, adding that the best they can do is to symbolize truths which one day our unclouded eyes will see in their full splendor while the best humans can do in arriving at the truth is to judge by the general drift of the messages (Moses 1924).

Moses wondered how he could be sure that Imperator and his band were not evil spirits—wolves in sheep's clothing—attempting to lead him astray, especially since some of the messages were contrary to Christian dogma. "Friend, you must discriminate between God's truth and man's glosses," Imperator counseled. "We do not dishonour the Lord Jesus—before whose exalted majesty we bow—by refusing to acquiesce in a fiction which He would disown, and which man has forced upon His name" (Moses 1924). Imperator went on to explain that the Spirit of Christ was the highest that could descend on earth and that He incarnated Himself in order to regen-

William Stainton Moses (standing), Dr. Speer
(seated), and the spirit form of "Rector" to their left.

erate the human race. However, Imperator took issue with the "crude human view" that made out God to be a cruel tyrant who needed to be propitiated by His Son's death, referring to the doctrine of the atonement as a "foul falsehood, degrading to God, degrading to that pure and stainless Spirit, to whom such things were falsely attributed, and misleading souls who rest on blind faith, and falsely imagine their credulity would be accounted a virtue" (*Meilach.com*).

As for the resurrection, Imperator told the sitters that Christ's resurrected body was a materialized spirit body and He appeared only to His own friends when conditions were perfect. The three archangels, Gabriel, Michael, and Raphael, concerned with governing the life of Jesus, removed the body, just as they had the body of the biblical Moses. The twelve apostles all had the gift of mediumship and were selected by Jesus for that reason. In the same way, the biblical Moses was commanded to choose seventy elders with mediumistic powers. "The return of the Christ is a spiritual fact, but a material age has come to regard it as a material fact, and to imagine that His physical body, having been transported into a material place called Heaven, will hereafter return in a material form to judge the quick and the dead" (*Meilach.com*).

On March 30, 1873, spirit messages started coming through Moses's hand by means of "automatic writing." This method was adopted, Moses was informed, for convenience purposes and so that he could preserve a connected body of teaching. Initially, the writing was very small and irregular, and it was necessary for Moses to write slowly and cautiously. However, the writing quickly became more regular and more legible. Most of the early messages came from Doctor, but after a time others started using Moses's hand. Each was distinguished by a different handwriting as well as peculiarities of style and expression. When some spirits found that they could not influence Moses's hand, they called upon Rector for assistance. Rector even acted as an amanuensis for Imperator. In 1883, Moses compiled his writing into a book entitled Spirit Teachings.

In order to avoid having his own thoughts conflict with those of the communicating spirit, Moses cultivated the ability to read an abstruse book while his hand was controlled by the spirit. "I never could command the writing," Moses wrote. "It came unsought usually; and when I did seek it, as often as not I was unable to obtain it. A sudden impulse, coming I knew not how, led me to sit down and prepare to write. Where the messages were in regular course, I was accustomed to devote the first hour of each day to sitting for their reception" (Moses 1924). Moses would usually put questions to the spirit at the beginning of the session and then start reading his book while waiting for answers.

As an experiment, Moses asked Rector if he would go to the bookcase and provide the last paragraph on page ninety-four of the last book on the second shelf. Moses did not check to see which book this might be. Rector responded (through Moses's hand) with what Moses would verify as the exact wording. As something of a reverse test, Rector, again using Moses's hand, wrote: "Pope is the last great writer of that school of poetry, the poetry of the intellect, or rather of the intellect mingled with fancy" (Moses 1924). He then told Moses to take the eleventh book on the same shelf and it would open at the proper page for him. Moses followed his instructions. The book opened at page 145 and there was the quotation.

On March 25, 1874, while the circle was receiving messages from Rector, a spirit giving her name as Charlotte Buckworth interrupted. She was unknown to any of the group. The next day, Moses, during an automatic writing session, asked about her. Rector explained that she had no special connection with the Imperator band, but due to unfavorable conditions which they were unable to harmonize, Buckworth was able to break in, and they allowed her to communicate. Rector informed Moses that Charlotte Buckworth had passed into spirit in 1773 as a result of heart problems increased by violent dancing at a party. She had just recently been brought within the earth's atmosphere and was attracted to circles where harmony prevails. Later, Moses checked a copy of the Annual Register for 1773 and verified Buckworth's existence and the cause of her death.

On another occasion, a spirit called Blanche Abercromby communicated through Moses's hand that she had "just quitted the body." Although Moses knew her, she lived some two hundred miles from London and he was unaware of her passing. Additional messages, in Abercrombie's own handwriting, came a few days later, but they were private and Moses made no mention of them to anyone. After Moses's death in 1892, researcher Frederic Myers was allowed to examine his papers. He came upon the Abercromby messages and wrote to her son for a sample of her handwriting. Both the son and a handwriting expert confirmed that messages received through Moses's hand were in Abercromby's handwriting.

One of Moses's earliest questions for Imperator had to do with the purpose of his mediumship, as he felt that the obstacles to reception of the messages by the majority of people were simply too great. The reply came, in effect, saying that the "river of God's truth" starts with little streams flowing into it.

Imperator and others often spoke of antagonistic spirits who were opposing their mission. "Such are powerful for mischief, and their activity shows itself in evil passion, in imitating our work, and so gaining influence over the deluded, and most of all, in presenting to inquiring souls that which is mean and base, where we would tenderly lead to the noble and refined," Imperator explained, going on to point out that as the soul lives in the earth-life, so does it go to spirit life (Moses 1924). The soul's tastes, predilections, habits, and antipathies remain with the soul and those with low morals and tastes—the earthbound spirits—frequent the haunts of their old vices while hovering around those who indulge in similar base pleasures, influencing them and gloating with fiendish glee as they succumb to further temptation. There are missionary spirits, Imperator added, that are constantly working with these earthbound spirits, but progress is often slow.

Still, Moses continued to doubt and resist some of the teachings. "We hail your doubts as the best evidence of our successful dealing with you," Imperator told him, adding that there is a point beyond which it is impossible to provide evidence. He called for Moses to use the standards of Jesus, "By their fruits shall ye know them" and "Men do not gather grapes of thorns, or figs of thistles," further telling him that he must consider the whole tenor of their teachings for proof that it is Divine (Moses 1924). For *definite* proof, Imperator continued, Moses must be content to wait until he too stood in their company. The most they could hope for is the gradual establishment of conviction. "We desire that you should apply to us the same law by which the Master judged—the Divine law of judging others as you would yourself be judged" (Moses 1924).

Moses continually asked for the earthly identifications of Imperator and the others. Imperator initially refused, informing Moses that revealing their earthly names would result in casting additional doubt on the validity of the messages. However, Imperator later revealed their names, advising Moses that they should not be mentioned in the book he would write. It was not until after Moses's death that the identities were made public by A. W. Trethewy in a book, *The Controls of Stainton Moses*. Imperator was Malachias, the Old Testament prophet. Rector was Hippolytus and Doctor was Athenodorus. Imperator took directions from Preceptor, who was Elijah. Preceptor, in turn, communed directly with Jesus. Other communicators in the band of forty-nine included Daniel, Ezekiel, John the Baptist, Solon, Plato, Aristotle, Seneca, Plotinus, Alexander Achillini, Algazzali, Kabbila, Chom, Said, Roophal, and Magus.

The character and integrity of Moses was such that all who observed the phenomena were certain that there was no trickery behind it. Charlton Speer described Moses as a man who loved truth, purity, and integrity, a man of absolute fearlessness and large-heartedness, and a man whose character was absent pride, fanaticism, arrogance, and conceit. Moreover, he was a man who avoided attention or publicity. "A wholesome skepticism is desirable, but to attribute imbecility or hallucination to eminent and cautious scientific investigators, or fraud to men of high intelligence and probity like the Rev. Stainton Moses is simply puerile," Sir William Barrett wrote in 1917 (Barrett 1917).

Frederic W. H. Myers, referred to by Professor William James, the eminent Harvard psychologist and philosopher, as the man who planted the flag of genuine science on psychical research, called Moses a "man of honor." Myers recalled the day, May 9, 1874, he and fellow psychical researcher Edmund Gurney first met Moses. "Standing as we were in the attitude natural at the commencement of such inquiries, under such conditions as were then attainable, an attitude of curiosity tempered by a vivid perception of difficulty and drawback, we now met a man of university education, of manifest sanity and probity, who vouched to us for a series of phenomena…He spoke frankly and fully; he showed his notebooks; he referred us to his friends; he inspired a belief which was at once sufficient, to prompt action" (Myers 1961).

It was suggested to Moses by some psychical researchers that all of the messages might have come from his subconscious mind without his being aware of it. But there were so many messages outside of the scope of his education and life experiences as well as in opposition to his beliefs that he could simply not accept such a recondite theory. "Spirits these people call themselves, having an existence independent of my life and consciousness," he wrote in 1889, three years before his death, "and, as such, I accept them" (*Meilach.com*).

Spirit Teachings Communicated through the Rev. William Stainton Moses

Here are some messages from Imperator and the band of forty-nine, as set forth in Spirit Teachings, published in 1883 (page number shown in parentheses)

Truth: "The Truth will always be esoteric. It must be so; for only to the soul that is prepared can it be given. Its fragrance is too evanescent for daily common use. Its subtle perfume is shed only in the inner chamber of spirit" (283).

Knowing Truth: "Hence, the days will never come to your world when all equally will know the Truth. There will always be many for whom it has no charms, for whom it would be fraught with danger to tread the upward paths of progress, and who prefer the beaten track worn by the feet of those who have trod it through the ages past" (281).

Death: "You forget that death leads to resurrection, and on to regenerated life—life in a wider sphere, with extended usefulness, with nobler aims,

Frederic W. H. Myers.

with truer purpose. You forget that death must precede such life—that what you call death, so far as it can affect Divine Truth, is but the dying of the grain of seed which is the condition of abundant increase. Death in life is the spiritual motto. Death culminating in a higher life. Victory in the grave, and through death. In dealing with spiritual truth do not forget this" (267).

Knowing God: "We have frequently said that God reveals Himself as man can bear it. It must be so. He is revealed through a human medium, and can only be made known in such measure as the medium can receive the communication. It is impossible that knowledge of God should outstrip man's capacity. Were we now to tell you—if we could—of our more perfect theology it would seem strange and unintelligible" (94).

Wrathful God: "We tell you nothing of such a God—a God of whom reason cannot think without a shudder, and from whom the fatherly instinct must shrink in disgust. Of this God of Love, who shows His life in such a fashion, we know nothing. He is of man's fashioning, unknown to us" (76).

Religion: "Ah, friend, religion is not so abstruse a problem as man has made it. It is comprised within narrow limits for the intelligence that is domiciled on earth. And the theological speculations, the dogmatic definitions with which man has overlaid the revelation of God, serve but to perplex and bewilder, and to involve the spirit struggling up to light in the mists and fogs of ignorance and superstition" (83).

Faith: "Blind faith can be no substitute for reasoning trust. For the faith is faith that either has grounds for its trust or not" (52).

Adversity: "It is necessary that afflictions come. Jesus knew and taught that. It is necessary for the training of the soul. It is as necessary as physical discipline for the body. No deep knowledge is to be had without it. None is permitted to scale the glorious heights but after discipline of sorrow. The key of knowledge is in spirit hands, and none may wrest it to himself but the earnest soul which is disciplined by trial" (280).

Jesus: "The human body of Jesus was of the most ethereal and perfect nature, and it was trained and prepared during 30 years of seclusion, for the three years of active work that the spirit had to do. It is very frequently, as in the case of Jesus of Nazareth, the after-effect of the life that is the truest part of the work" (250).

Spirit evolution: "Yea, even the deeds done in the body have their issue in the life disembodied. Their outcome is not bounded by the barrier which you call death. Far otherwise; for the condition of the spirit at its inception of its real life is determined by the outcome of its bodily acts. The spirit which has been slothful or impure gravitates necessarily to its congenial sphere, and commences there a period of probation which has its object the purification of the spirit from the accumulated habits of its earth life; the remedying in remorse and shame of the evil done; and the gradual raising of itself to a higher state towards which each process of purification has been a step. This is the punishment of transgression, not an arbitrary doom inflicted to all eternity by an angry God, but the inevitable doom of remorse and repentance and retribution, which results invariably from conscious sin" (157).

Spirit influence: "Advanced spirits influence the thoughts, suggest ideas, furnish means of acquiring knowledge, and of communicating it to mankind. The ways by which spirits so influence men are manifold. They have means that you know not of by which events are so arranged as to work out the end they have in view" (35).

Obstacles to spirit influence: "Men become absorbed in the material, that which they can see, and grasp, and hoard up, and they forget that there is a future and spirit life. They become so earthly that they are impervious to our influence; so material that we cannot come near them; so full of earthly interests that there is no room for that which will endure when they have passed away" (39).

Continuation of marriage ties: "That depends entirely on similarity of taste and equality of development…The spirits can progress side by side. In our state we know only of community of taste and of association between those who are on the same plane and can be developed by mutual help…There can be no community of interest save between congenial souls…Spirits filled with mutual love can never be really separated. You are hampered in understanding our state by considerations of time and space" (45).

Heaven: "No fabled dreamy heaven of eternal inactivity awaits you, but a sphere of progressive usefulness and growth to higher perfection" (77).

Judgment: "Is it nothing that we tell you that reward and punishment are not delayed till a far-off day faintly imagined, after a period of torpor, almost of death, but are instant, immediate, supervening upon sin by the action of an invariable law, and acting ceaselessly until the cause which produced it is removed?" (121).

Pseudo-Science: "The pseudo-scientific man, who will look at nothing save through his own medium, and on his own terms—who will deal with us only so that he may be allowed to prescribe means of demonstrating us to be deluders, liars, figments of a disordered brain—he is of little moment to us. His blinded eye cannot see, and his cloudy intelligence, befogged and cramped with lifelong prejudice, can be of little service to us" (49).

Five

Sir William Barrett
Investigates Strange Phenomena

Sooner or later psychical research will demonstrate to the educated world, not only the existence of a soul in man, but also the existence of a soul in Nature.

– Sir William Barrett

Before Professor William F. Barrett began exploring the world of psychic phenomena in 1874, he was convinced that the seemingly ridiculous stories he had heard about raps, taps, tabletilting, materializations, and spirit communication were all the result of mal-observation or some type of hallucination. A professor of physics at the Royal College of Science in Dublin, Barrett had served as assistant to Professor John Tyndall, the famous physicist, during his days as a student. "The atmosphere surrounding my early years there was entirely opposed to any belief in psychical phenomena," Barrett said in a 1924 talk before the Society for Psychical Research (SPR) in London, adding that his mechanistic outlook was also influenced by another famous scientist, Michael Faraday, who provided him much guidance (Barrerrt 1986).

Barrett went on to become a distinguished scientist in his own right, developing a silicon-iron alloy known as stalloy, used in the commercial development of the telephone and transformers, while also doing pioneering research on entoptic vision, leading to the invention of the entoptiscope and a new optometer. In 1912, he was knighted for his scientific work and became Sir William Barrett.

In 1874, when he was twenty-nine years old, Barrett began experimenting with hypnosis, then more popularly known as "mesmerism." He observed a young girl under hypnosis correctly identify a playing card taken randomly from a pack and placed in a book that was put next to her head. He also observed another hypnotized person correctly identifying fourteen cards taken at random from a pack. As a scientist, he found such results very disturbing. However, while many of his scientific colleagues simply scoffed at anything paranormal, Barrett was open-minded and determined to find some rational and scientific explanation. As Barrett explained in that 1924 talk as well as in his 1917 book *On the Threshold of the Unseen,* his prior theories really began to fall apart sometime in 1876 when a prominent English solicitor (lawyer) named Clark spent the summer at a residence near his in Dublin.

"They were not spiritualists and were puzzled and somewhat annoyed by the raps and other inexplicable noises that frequently occurred when their daughter Florrie was present," Barrett wrote, going on to explain that Mr. and Mrs. Clark at first thought their ten-year-old daughter was playing some kind of childish trick on them (Barrett 1917). When the child's governess and music mistress reported similar rappings in different parts of the child's school as they observed Florrie idle or playing the piano, they became especially concerned and requested Barrett's assistance in determining a cause.

At 10 o'clock on a bright summer morning, Barrett sat down with Florrie and her parents at a large dining table with no cloth on it. He sat in a position where he could easily see Florrie's hands and feet. While her hands

Sir William F. Barrett.

and feet remained absolutely motionless, Barrett heard raps on the table and on the back of their chairs. "The noise was exactly as would be made by hammering small nails into the floor, and my first thought was that some carpenters were in the room above or below, but on examination no one was there," Barrett continued the story. "We found the raps grew in intensity when a merry song was stuck up, or music was played, the raps in a most amusing way keeping time with the music, occasionally changing to a loud rhythmic scraping, as if the bow of a cello were drawn on a piece of wood" (Barrett 1917). Barrett placed his ear on the spot from which the "rough fiddling" seemed to emanate and distinctly felt the rhythmic vibration going on in the table. However, he could not detect any cause either above or below the table. At times, the raps traveled away and were heard in different parts of the room not near anyone present.

Aware of the stories that there is an "intelligence" causing such raps and that this invisible intelligence might be able to communicate, Barrett told the intelligence that he would slowly recite the alphabet and asked "it" to respond with a rap at letters that might spell out a message. In such a way, Barrett identified the communicator as a young boy named "Walter Hussey." Apparently, the name meant nothing to Florrie or her parents, although Mrs. Clark reported overhearing Florrie having animated conversations with an invisible companion after putting her to bed on a number of occasions

Barrett asked "Walter" to rap at a small table away from Florrie. Walter complied. Barrett called in other observers and, inasmuch as they all heard the rappings, he discounted his hallucination theory. As there was a popular debunking theory that raps were the result of the medium slipping the toe or knee joints in and out with a click, Barrett asked Florrie to put her hands flat against the wall and stretch her feet away from the wall as far as she could, thereby making muscular movement virtually impossible. The raps continued and he eliminated that theory. Barrett described all of the communication from Walter as "merry and meaningless."

Movement of furniture also took place around Florrie. "On one occasion, in full sunlight when seated with Mr. and Mrs. Clark and Florrie at the large mahogany dining table, big enough to seat twelve at dinner, all our fingers visibly resting on the tops of the table, suddenly three legs of the table deliberately rose off the floor to a height sufficient to enable me to put my foot beneath the castors," Barrett continued, adding that such a feat was well beyond the strength of any child (Barrett 1917).

After the Clark family had returned to England, Barrett was informed by Mr. Clark that there were some manifestations there more violent than any Barrett had witnessed. They continued to be of a meaningless or frivolous nature. However, they gradually died away.

As a result of his experiments in hypnosis and his investigation of Florrie Clark, Barrett prepared a paper to deliver to the British Association for the Advancement of Science. The Association rejected the paper as well as Barrett's request to present it orally to the group. After Alfred Russel Wallace, co-originator with Charles Darwin of the natural selection theory of evolution, protested the Association's action, Barrett was allowed to deliver the paper but not to publish it.

In his 1917 book, Barrett related another case of rapping, this one by a "Miss L.," a Dublin resident whose family was quite upset by the phenomena. Sitting with Miss L. under bright gas light, Barrett was startled by loud raps. Holding his hand out of the sight of Miss L., Barrett tested the invisible intelligence by asking "it" to tell him how many fingers he was holding up. The correct number was rapped out. On a second try, the number was again correct. It also spelled out messages as Barrett recited the alphabet. Barrett asked the intelligence if "it" could levitate the table, and "it" responded by raising the table eight to ten inches off the ground. When Barrett moved his chair away from the table, the table followed him and imprisoned him in his seat. Barrett observed the table rising repeatedly and was able to confirm that Miss L. was in no way touching it and that there were no invisible threads, as skeptics had suggested in other cases of levitation. He also had Miss L. come to his own home to repeat the phenomena and recorded that the table moved about so violently that he had to stop the performance, fearing that it would damage the chandelier in the room below.

In still another case, Barrett was invited by Dr. William J. Crawford, a lecturer on mechanical engineering at Queen's University in Belfast, to observe the phenomena produced by a seventeen-year-old girl named Kathleen Goligher, whom Crawford had been studying for some six months. In clear light, a group sat around a small table with hands joined together. Very soon, knocks came and messages were delivered when the alphabet was recited. Then the table began to rise from the floor some eighteen inches and remain suspended long enough for Barrett to observe that no one was touching it. "I tried to press the table down, and though I exerted all my strength could not do so," Barrett wrote of the sitting. "Then I climbed up on the table and sat on it, my feet off the floor, when I was swayed to and fro and finally tipped off. The table on its own accord now turned upside down, no one touching it, and I tried to lift it off the ground, but it could not be stirred, it appeared screwed down to the floor" (Barrett 1917).

When Barrett stopped trying to lift the inverted table from the floor, it righted itself on its own accord, everyone else in the room standing well clear of it. "Numerous sounds displaying an amused intelligence then came, and after each individual present had been greeted with some farewell raps the sitting ended" (Barrett 1917).

Some years later, beginning around 1912, Barrett observed and participated in a number of sittings with a small private circle of his Dublin friends who were experimenting with the Ouija board. They included Hester (Dowden) Travers Smith, the oldest daughter of Professor Edward Dowden, a Shakespearian scholar Lennox Robinson, a world-renowned Irish playwright and the Rev. Savill Hicks, M.A. Two members of the group would sit blindfolded at the board, their fingers lightly touching the board's "traveler," a triangular piece of wood which flies from letter to letter under the direction of a "control" (a spirit communicating directly or relaying messages from other spirits unable to directly communicate), while a third person copied the messages letter by letter. At times the traveler moved so rapidly that it was necessary to record the messages in shorthand. Although Barrett had no doubt as to the honesty and integrity of his friends, he designed special eye-patches for them to wear so that there could be no question as to them seeing where the traveler was pointing. On one occasion he turned the board around to see if the results would be the same. They were. On another occasion, to sat-

Kathleen Goligher.

isfy a skeptical observer, who theorized that the blindfolded operators had memorized the position of the letters on the board, the letters were rearranged and a screen was put between the two operators, who remained blindfolded. Still, coherent messages came.

When Barrett asked the controlling spirit if any friend of his could send a message, he heard from a deceased friend, who communicated a message for the Dublin Grand Lodge of Freemasons, of which he (the spirit) had been a high-ranking member. Barrett was reasonably certain that neither of the board operators was aware of the friend's Masonic affiliation.

On another occasion, Barrett sat at the board, securely blindfolded. He reported that he was startled by the "extraordinary vigor, decision, and swiftness with which the indicator moved." A message came through that Barrett was not suited for receiving. In other words, he did not have the mediumistic psychic power necessary to adequately receive messages.

One of the more interesting cases reported by Barrett is referred to as "The Pearl Tie-Pin Case." Hester Travers Smith was sitting at the board with a "Miss C.," the daughter of a physician. The name of Miss C's cousin, an army officer killed in France a month earlier, was unexpectedly spelled out on the board and then the message came: "Tell mother to give my pearl tie-pin to the girl I was going to marry, I think she ought to have it." As Miss C. was unaware that her cousin had intended to marry and did not know the name of the woman, she asked that the name and address of the woman be given. The full Christian and surname was given on the board along with an address in London. Either the address was not accurately communicated or was taken down wrong as a letter sent to that address was returned. Miss C. checked with other family members and none was aware that the cousin had been engaged nor knew the fiancée named.

Several months later, the family of the young officer received his personal effects from the War Office. They included a pearl tie-pin along with a will naming the fiancée as his next of kin. Both the Christian and surname were exactly as given to Miss C.

It was Barrett who encouraged three Cambridge intellectuals—Frederic W. H. Myers, Henry Sidgwick, and Edmund Gurney, all classical scholars—to form the Society for Psychical Research (SPR) in 1882. Before becoming a professor of moral philosophy, Sidgwick had, around 1853, joined a group called the Ghost Society, formed in 1851 by his cousin, Edward White Benson, later Archbishop of Canterbury, and began collecting records of paranormal phenomena. In 1860, Myers went to Trinity College to read classics, and Sidgwick became his tutor. The two became good friends, often discussing philosophical matters. Both Myers and Gurney were significantly moved by observing the mediumship of the Rev. William Stainton Moses in 1874. Apparently, because Barrett was living in Dublin, he could not take an active part in the early leadership of the SPR, but he is considered the man most responsible for the organization.

"I am personally convinced," Barrett said in his 1924 talk before the SPR, "that the evidence we have published decidedly demonstrates (1) the existence of a spiritual world, (2) survival after death, and (3) of occasional communication from those who have passed over" (Barrett 1986).

Six

Myers Communicates from the Other Side

If Myers was not a mystic, he had all the faith of a mystic and the ardour of an apostle, in conjunction with the sagacity and precision of a savant.

—Dr. Charles Richet

Although not educated as a psychologist, Frederic W. H. Myers, one of the founders of the Society for Psychical Research (SPR), has been credited with developing a systematic conception of the subliminal self as well as a theory holding that telepathy is one of the basic laws of life. In fact, it was Myers who coined the word "telepathy," previously called "thought-transference." University of Geneva psychology professor Theodor Flournoy, also a psychical researcher during Myers's time, opined that Myer's name should be joined to those of Copernicus and Darwin, completing "the triad of geniuses" who most profoundly revolutionized scientific thought.

According to Dr. Sherwood Eddy, a distinguished American writer of the first half of the last century, Myers began to explore the subconscious, or subliminal self, simultaneous with and independently of Freud. While Freud accepted atomic materialism, seeing the spirit world as mere wishful

thinking and religion as outright fraud, Myers concluded that the Power
behind the universe is super-organic, in a higher category to which human
personality belongs. He saw psychical research as a meeting place of religion, philosophy, and science. Since materialism had, in the wake of Darwinism, become the "intelligent" approach, Myers's view did not gain wide-
spread acceptance and he is not well remembered today.

Born in Keswick, Cumberland, England, on February 6, 1843, Myers,
the son of a clergyman, graduated from Trinity College, Cambridge in 1864,
then became a classical lecturer at Cambridge and a fellow of Trinity. By
1869, he had, like most Cambridge intellectuals, lost his faith and, concomitantly, his belief in the survival of consciousness at death. Myers wrote that
his agnosticism or virtual materialism affected him like "a dull pain borne
with joyless doggedness, sometimes a shock of nightmare-panic amid the
glaring dreariness of the day." He felt that the hope of the world was van-
ishing, not his alone. His interest in psychical research was sparked during
the 1870s by the mediumship of the Reverend William Stainton Moses, then
fueled by the mediumship of Leonora Piper. After joining with Henry Sidgwick, Edmund Gurney, and William Barrett in organizing the SPR in 1882,
he collaborated with Gurney and Frank Podmore in authoring *Phantasms
of the Living*.

Myers's seminal work, *Human Personality and Its Survival of Bodily
Death*, was published in 1903, two years after his death. "In the long story
of man's endeavors to understand his own environment and to govern his
own fate, there is one gap or omission so singular that its simple statement
has the air of paradox," Myers begins the Introduction of the book. "Yet, it
is strictly true to say that man has never yet applied the methods of modern science to the problem which most profoundly concerns him—whether
or not his personality involves any element which can survive bodily death"
(Myers 1961).

As Myers saw it, telepathy is a law prevailing in the spiritual as well as
the material world. He felt that there was sufficient evidence to conclude

that those who communicated with us telepathically in this world could continue to communicate telepathically from the other world.

Harvard professor William James called Myers the pioneer (of psychical research) who planted the flag of genuine science upon the field. Sir Oliver Lodge, the distinguished British physicist and radio pioneer, stated that Myers had been laying the foundation for a cosmic philosophy. It was Myers, Lodge explained, who broke down his skepticism and showed him the reasonableness of the survival hypothesis.

Between 1898 and 1900, Myers had over 150 sittings with British trance medium Rosalie Thompson, whose chief control was her deceased daughter, Nelly. Through Thompson, Myers received a number of convincing messages from his deceased cousin, Annie Marshall, who had committed suicide in 1876. He had earlier heard from her through the mediumship of Mrs. Piper. Those messages, more than anything else, convinced Myers of survival. According to Lodge, his close friend, Myers approached death with an absolute and childlike confidence that death was a mere physical event. "To him, it was an adversity which must happen to the body, but it was not one of those evil things which may assault and hurt the soul," Lodge said in a talk to the SPR shortly after Myers died, at age fifty-seven, on January 17, 1901, while in Rome (Lodge 1909).

On February 19, 1901, Lodge and his wife were sitting with Rosalie Thompson when Thompson went into a trance and Nelly began speaking through her. She said that she first saw Myers on February 6, his birthday, but she did not believe that he had actually passed over to her side. She thought she was seeing him in some kind of vision. However, she quickly realized that he had in fact made his transition. Nelly tried to get Myers to communicate with Lodge, but said that he was not fully awakened. She asked Lodge to try again in two hours, during which time she would attempt to awaken him. Thompson came out of her trance at 6:30 p.m., then returned to the trance state after dinner, at 8:30. Nelly brought Myers, who struggled to communicate. "Lodge, it is not as easy as I thought in my impatience,"

Myers said. "Gurney [who had died in 1888] says I am getting on first rate. But I am short of breath" (Lodge 1909).

Myers went on to say that he was confused when he first arrived on the other side, before he realized he was dead. "I thought I had lost my way in a strange town, and I groped my way along the passage," he said. "And even when I saw people that I knew were dead, I thought they were only visions. I have not seen Tennyson yet by the way" (Lodge 1909).

Myers continued, explaining that in attempting to visualize the surroundings at the Lodge home during the sitting, it was if he were looking at a misty picture. He could hear himself using Thompson's voice, but he didn't feel like it was his "whole self" talking. He said he was having a difficult time in remembering things. In fact, he could not recall his mother's name. When Lodge asked him about the SPR, Myers could not recall anything about the organization. Nelly took over her mother's entranced mechanism and explained that Myers was still in a state of confusion and would remember a great deal more in time.

On May 8, 1901, Lodge and his wife again sat with Thompson. Nelly communicated and said that she had not seen Myers since they put the "umbrella" up. Lodge did not understand what was meant by that, but some weeks later, after hearing about a purported message delivered by Gurney on February 7, 1901, through a medium referred to as Miss Rawson, the umbrella reference made sense. Gurney, who was apparently assisting Myers in adapting to his new environment, said that too many people were calling upon Myers and it was interfering with his rest. "What we want for him now is to rise, and to forget earthly things," Gurney said through Miss Rawson, going on to explain that if people continued trying to communicate with Myers that he would be forced to hover near the earth plane, thereby making him earthbound (Lodge 1909). Thus, the "umbrella" was apparently put up by Gurney and other friends on that side to shield Myers from the demands being placed upon him by people trying to communicate with him—those who had come to recognize him as a leader in the field of psy-

Sir Oliver Lodge.

chical research.

Nelly further told Lodge that there was too much "undercurrent of suspicion" on his (Lodge's) part and that this "befogged" her. He needed to be more sympathetic for her to give him things. Lodge tried to reassure her that he was not trying to be hostile and would do his best to overcome what doubts he had. Perhaps because Lodge and Myers were good friends, Nelly was able to get through the "umbrella" and bring Myers to speak. But Lodge recorded that the speech coming from Thompson's vocal cords was very feeble and confused, much of it gibberish, at least what he could make out. Yet, he was able to understand and record a number of things during the hour and a half sitting.

Myers repeated that communicating was much harder than he had realized when he was in his earthly shell. "Lodge, it is just as they say, you grope in fog and darkness," Myers said. "They keep on calling me. I am wanted everywhere. I hear them calling, and I cannot tell who it is at first…I want to concentrate in a few places, or in one place, and not to be split up…Do appeal to them not to break me up so, and leave me not clear in one spot…How easy to promise and how difficult to fulfill" (Lodge 1909).

Nelly took over from Myers and said that her mother (Thompson) was calling Myers too often, not allowing him the proper rest. She added that Myers informed her that some communication purportedly coming from him was not from him, and yet it was not fraud. He said he didn't understand it yet and so couldn't explain it. He added that others informed him that when he (Myers) was in the flesh and thought he was receiving messages from a particular spirit it was not them. And yet they knew about it, and it was not fraud. "He does not know how it is worked, but he is study-ing, and he thinks it will help a great deal if he can understand how the cheating things that are not cheats are done," Nelly said. "It is not cheating, and yet it is not him doing it…" (Lodge 1909).

Lodge later learned that during the last half hour of his sitting with Thompson, Margaret Verrall, an automatic-writing medium as well as a member of the SPR, was attempting to receive messages from Myers. Among the few words she was able to get were: "No power," and "Doing something else tonight" (Lodge 1909).

Meanwhile, researchers in the United States were getting equally disappointing messages from Myers through Mrs. Piper. More than two years later, on September 19, 1903, Alice MacDonald Fleming, the sister of author Rudyard Kipling, began receiving automatic writing messages purportedly coming from Myers. Fleming, the wife of a British army officer, was living in India at the time. Because members of her family disapproved of her "dabbling in the occult," she used the pseudonym "Mrs. Holland." The initial messages were short and apparently an attempt by Myers to convince her of his identity. He told her that much of what he would write through her was not meant for her, that she was to be the reporter. She was asked by Myers to send the messages to the SPR in London.

In a subsequent message, Myers told Fleming not to worry about being made a fool or dupe. "It's a form of restless vanity to fear that your hand is imposing upon yourself, as it were," Myers communicated to her. To the SPR (through Fleming), he communicated: "…if it were possible for the soul to die back into earth life again I should die from sheer yearning to reach you— to tell you that all that we imagined is not half wonderful enough for the truth…If I could only reach you—if I could only tell you—I long for power and all that comes to me is an infinite yearning—an infinite pain. Does any of this reach you—reaching anyone—or am I only wailing as the wind wails—wordless and unheeded?" (Holt 1914).

On January 5, 1904, Myers wrote that he was in a "bound to earth condition," but it was largely of a voluntary choice. "I am, as it were, actuated by the missionary spirit; and the great longing to speak to the souls in prison—still in the prison of flesh—leads me to 'absent me from felicity awhile'" (Lodge 1909).

On another occasion, Myers wrote that "to believe that the mere act of death enables a spirit to understand the whole mystery of death is as absurd as to imagine that the act of birth enables an infant to understand the whole mystery of life." He added that he was still groping…surmising… conjecturing (Barrett 1917).

Fleming also received messages from Edmund Gurney and Roden Noel, both unknown to her. A message from Noel said to ask "A.W." what the date May 26, 1894, meant to him, and if he could not remember, to ask Nora. Not knowing what to make of the message, Fleming sent the message to the SPR in London, where it was recognized that Noel was referring to Noel's good friends, Dr. A. W. Verrall and Dr. Eleanor (Nora) Sidgwick. The date was the day of his death.

On January 17, 1904, Fleming recorded another message purportedly coming from Myers for the SPR. He gave the biblical reference "I Cor. xvi, 12." He told the SPR that he tried to get the entire wording through in Greek but could not get Fleming's hand to form Greek characters, and so he gave only the reference. On the very same day, thousands of miles away in England, Mrs. Verrall also received the same biblical reference from Myers by means of automatic writing. This biblical passage, "Watch ye, stand fast in the faith, quit you like men, be strong," was the wording inscribed in Greek over the gateway of Selwyn College, Cambridge, under which Myers frequently passed.

This was apparently the first of what came to be known as the "cross-correspondences"—similar messages through different mediums around the world or fragmentary messages sent through different mediums which in themselves had no meaning until the SPR linked them up and made a complete message out of them. Fleming ("Mrs. Holland") in India, Piper in the United States, Verrall, and Winifred Coombe-Tenant ("Mrs. Willett"), both in England, were the four principal mediums used by Myers in delivering these cross-correspondences. As Myers was a classical scholar, a number of the messages had to do with the classics.

While complex and very difficult to read, these cross-correspondences are often looked upon as the best evidence of survival of individual consciousness after death. "The intention was obvious—namely to show that one mind was acting on all these mediums," Lodge explained, "each separate portion of the message being so obscure that there could be no telepathy or any other means of communication between them" (Lodge 1932).

On December 20, 1905, Anne Manning Robbins was having a sitting with Piper. Her long-time friend Augustus P. Martin was communicating with her and mentioned that some "man" named Myer or Myers had been anxiously hanging around hoping to use the "light" (Piper's body), but apparently became discouraged and left. This had happened, he said, on several occasions. Martin described him as a "very active, brilliant, fine man, keen perceptions, finest type of mind." Whether it was Frederic Myers or not was not determined, but Manning was reasonably certain that Martin knew nothing of Myers when he was alive.

By 1924, Myers must have felt that he had given as much proof of his existence as possible as he then began delivering more profound messages concerning life after death through the mediumship of Geraldine Cummins of Ireland. As Myers had died when Cummins was a small child, she knew very little about him and had not read his book, *Human Personality and its Survival of Bodily Death*. Yet, while sitting with her friend, Beatrice Gibbs, an SPR member, one day, Cummins's hand wrote the name "Frederic Myers" and "good morning." Over the next seven years, Myers attempted to communicate information about life on his side of the veil. He told of seven planes or spheres forming the ladder of consciousness. In the seventh plane, the spirit and its various souls become fused and pass into the Supreme Mind. "This merging with the Idea, with the Great Source of spirit does not imply annihilation," he wrote. "You still exist as an individual. You are as a wave in the sea; and you have at last entered into Reality and cast from you all the illusions of appearance" (Cummins 1932). He went on to say that it baffles description and that he found it "heartbreaking" to attempt to write of it.

Part II

Chapters 7–10

The Mediumship of Leonora Piper, "The White Crow"

Until within very recent years, the scientific world has tacitly rejected a large number of important philosophical conceptions on the ground that there is absolutely no evidence in their favor whatever. Among those popular conceptions are those of the essential independence of the mind and the body, of the existence of a supersensible world, and of the possibility of occasional communication between that world and this. We have here [in Mrs. Piper], as it seems to me, evidence that is worthy of consideration for all these points.

—William R. Newbold (1865–1926)
Professor of Philosophy, Univ. of Pennsylvania

Seven

Leonora Piper, the Most Tested Medium

Few persons have been so long and so carefully observed, and [Mrs. Piper] has left on all observers the impression of thorough uprightness, candor, and honesty.

—**Sir Oliver Lodge**

The most celebrated case of mediumship on record is that of Leonora Piper, a Boston housewife. She was discovered in 1885 by William James, the distinguished Harvard professor of psychology and philosophy, and was studied extensively by scientists and scholars representing both the British and American branches of the Society for Psychical Research (SPR). James referred to her as his "white crow," the one that upset the "law" that all crows are black—the one who proved that not all mediums are charlatans.

"This lady can at will pass into a trance condition in which she is 'controlled' by a power purporting to be the spirit of a French doctor, who serves as an intermediary between the sitter and the deceased friends," James reported to the American branch of the SPR in July 1886 (Holt 1914). The "French doctor" called himself Phinuit, telling one investigator that his full name was Jean Phinuit Sclivelle but that he was known when incarnate as

Dr. Phinuit. He further said that he died at age seventy in 1860.

"I am persuaded of the medium's honesty, and of the genuineness of her trance," James further reported, "and…I now believe her to be in possession of a power as yet unexplained" (Holt 1914).

Prominent author and publisher Henry Holt had several sittings with Piper. He related that after she had been seated a minute or two, her eyeballs rolled upward, her face became slightly convulsed, and she began talking in a rough voice not her own. He recalled the voice affecting him as if it were coming from a statue, "pouring forth at one moment some brusquerie in the rough deep tones of Phinuit; at the next, in the same voice softened to gentleness, petting a child; then, perhaps, a return to the gruff tones in some biting sarcasm to some interloping control; then perhaps issuing from the same mouth, a child's voice singing the little boat song—all going on amid the weeping relatives who join in the song" (Holt 1914).

After being told by his mother-in-law that she had sat with Piper and had been given much information about deceased relatives, Professor James became curious and decided to have his own sitting with her. He left his first sitting with Piper convinced that she either had supernormal powers or had somehow become acquainted with a great deal of his family's history. After a dozen sittings in which deceased relatives or friends communicated through her entranced body, James came to accept her supernormal powers, certain that she could not have known or researched all of the information that came through.

James learned that Piper had discovered her mediumistic ability in 1884 after being persuaded by her husband's father and mother to sit with Mr. J. R. Cocke, a blind healing medium, because of a tumor. He claimed to be controlled by a French physician named *Finny*. During her second sitting with Cocke, Piper, then twenty-seven, lost consciousness and was said to have been controlled by the spirit of a young Indian girl who gave the name Chlorine. Apparently, Finny was Phinuit (pronounced almost the same), who must have decided that Piper offered him a better "organism"

Leonora Piper.

than Cocke or decided to use both organisms.

According to James, Phinuit would often introduce other spirits and at times would give long lectures about things he (James) was certain were well beyond Piper's intellect. "The most remarkable thing about the Phinuit personality seems to me the extraordinary tenacity and minuteness of his memory," James further reported. "The medium has been visited by many hundreds of sitters, half of them, perhaps, being strangers who have come but once. To each Phinuit gives an hour full of disconnected fragments of talk about persons living, dead, or imaginary, and events past, future, or unreal. What normal waking memory could keep this chaotic mass of stuff together? Yet Phinuit does so…So far as I can discover, Mrs. Piper's waking memory is not remarkable, and the whole constitution of her trance-memory is something which I am at a loss to understand" (Holt 1914).

On September 6, 1888, J. Rogers Rich, an artist, had a sitting with Piper. He observed a remarkable change in her voice as it became unmistakably male and "rather husky." He was at once addressed in French and he responded in French. Dr. Phinuit diagnosed Rich's physical ailments for him and prescribed various herbs, giving the manner of preparing them. Phinuit told him that his mother was beside him and accurately described her. In a second sitting, a month later, Phinuit told Rich that his deceased niece was at his side. To test him, Rich asked the niece, who had lived all her life in France, for his name in French, to which Phinuit accurately relayed "Thames Rowghearce Reach" entirely in the French alphabet (Holt 1914).

In another sitting, Phinuit's foreign accent gave way to a pure English accent and Rich was greeted by his old friend, "Newell." Rich noted that the entranced Piper was twiddling her fingers as if twirling a mustache, a habit very characteristic of Newell.

In still another sitting, Rich was told by Phinuit that his sister was often in his surroundings and had much influence over him. Rich replied that he had never had a sister. Phinuit corrected him, saying that he had a sister who died in infancy before he was born. Rich questioned an aunt about this and was informed that it was true.

On December 28, 1888, the Rev. W. H. Savage, a friend of William James, sat with Piper. Phinuit told him that somebody named Robert West was there and wanted to send a message to Savage's brother. The message was in the form of an apology for something West had written about the brother "in advance." Savage did not understand the message but passed it on to his brother who understood it and explained that West was editor of a publication called *The Advance* and had criticized his work in an editorial. During the sitting, Savage asked for a description of West. An accurate description was given along with the information that West had died of hemorrhage of the kidneys, a fact unknown to Savage but later verified.

In a sitting by Savage two weeks later, West again communicated, stating that his body was buried at Alton, Illinois and giving the wording on his tombstone, "Fervent in spirit, serving the Lord" (Holt 1914). Savage was unaware of either of these facts, but later confirmed them as true.

After hearing about Piper from James, the SPR in England decided to invite her to their country to be tested. There, in late 1889, she had many sittings with Frederic W. H. Myers, the Cambridge scholar who co-founded the SPR, and Professor Oliver Lodge (later, Sir Oliver), the renowned physicist and radio pioneer.

In one sitting, Lodge handed the entranced Piper an old gold watch that had belonged to his deceased Uncle Jerry and which had been sent to him by his Uncle Robert, Jerry's twin brother. Lodge asked Phinuit if he could tell him anything about the watch. Phinuit immediately said it had belonged to one of Lodge's uncles. Shortly thereafter, the voice coming through Piper said, "This is my watch, and Robert is my brother, and I am here. Uncle Jerry, my watch" (Lodge 1909).

Even though Piper was in a trance, Lodge still considered telepathy, or mindreading, as an explanation for this, so he asked Uncle Jerry if he could recall some trivial details about his (Jerry's) boyhood—something unknown to him (Oliver) but known to his Uncle Robert. Uncle Jerry then recalled episodes of swimming a creek together and running a risk of getting drowned, killing a cat in Smith's field, the possession of a small rifle, and of a long peculiar skin, like a snake-skin, which he thought was now in the possession of Uncle Robert. Robert verified all but the killing of the cat, but he admitted that his memory was failing him. However, another brother, Frank, clearly recalled the cat-killing incident in Smith's field.

On December 21, 1889, Phinuit told Lodge that "Edmund sends his love." Then, the personality possessing Piper seemed to change and Edmund Gurney, who along with Myers and Professors William Barrett and Henry Sidgwick founded the SPR in 1882, began speaking. Gurney had died in 1888 and had been introduced to Lodge by Myers.

"I am here, I etherially exist," Gurney told Lodge. "I wrote to you about some books for the Society. I have seen a little woman that's a medium, a true medium. I have written to Myers using her hand. I did do it, I, Edmund Gurney, I" (Holt 1914). Lodge questioned Gurney about both Piper and Phinuit. Gurney told him that Piper was a true medium. As for Phinuit, he said, "He is not all one would wish, but he is all right." Gurney further told Lodge: "There is no death, only a shadow and then Light. Experiment and observations are indispensable. We have to use some method like this to communicate" (Holt 1914).

At a sitting four days later, Lodge recorded that Phinuit seemed to leave as Gurney again took over in a more educated voice. Lodge noted that the changeover took place with some uncertainty and difficulty and he could hear Phinuit giving *sotto voce* (whispered) instructions to Gurney before Gurney began speaking. Lodge again asked Gurney about Phinuit and Gurney responded by describing him as eccentric and quaint but good-hearted. "I wouldn't do the things he does for anything. He lowers himself sometimes; it's a great pity. He has very curious ideas about things and people, he receives a great deal about people from themselves…and he gets expressions and phrases that one doesn't care for, vulgar phrases he picks up by meeting uncanny people through the medium…A high type of man couldn't do the work he does" (Holt 1914).

Lodge asked Gurney to further explain how he communicated and if it was harmful to the medium. "It's the only way, Lodge," Gurney responded. "In one sense it's bad, but in another it is good. It is her work. If I take possession of the medium's body, and she goes out, then I can use her organism to tell the world important truths. There is an infinite power above us. Lodge, believe it fully, infinite over all, most marvelous." Gurney told Lodge that when he "passed out" he was confused and didn't know who he was or where he was. "I hunted about for my friends and for my body. Soon however my sister welcomed me. Three of them, all drowned" (Holt 1914).

In another sitting, Lodge's wife was present and when Lodge introduced her, the entranced Mrs. Piper reached out to greet her, Gurney continuing to speak and mentioning that he had tea with her once, which was true and certainly not known to Piper.

Lodge asked Gurney what constitutes a medium. "Not too much spirituality and not too much animalism, not the highest people and not the lowest," Gurney replied. "Sympathetic and not too self-conscious, able to let their minds be given up to another—that sort of person—easily influenced. Many could, but their pride and a sense of self comes in and spoils it" (Holt 1914).

On February 3, 1890, Gurney again discussed Phinuit, as if Phinuit had gone away. "Phinuit will be coming back soon," Gurney told Lodge. "He's a good old man. He has a hard place. I wouldn't do the work he does for anything. Seeing all manner of people and hunting up their friends, and often he has hard work to persuade them that they are really wanted." Lodge then asked Gurney if Phinuit is reliable. "Not perfectly, he is not a bit infallible. He mixes things terribly sometimes. He does his best; he's a good old man, but he does get confused, and when he can't hear distinctly he fills it up himself. He does invent things occasionally, he certainly does" (Holt 1914).

As for Phinuit's medical knowledge, Gurney told Lodge that he is a "shrewd doctor" who "knows his business thoroughly." He explained that Phinuit can see into people and is very keen on their complaints, but definitely not infallible. When Gurney told Lodge that he must be going, Piper returned to the Phinuit mannerisms.

While James, Lodge, Myers, and others investigated Piper, the principal investigator over the years was Dr. Richard Hodgson, an Australian who had been teaching philosophy at Cambridge University when he was recruited by the British branch of the SPR to investigate mediums. Highly skeptical of all mediums, he gave a negative report on Madame Blavatsky, thought to be a gifted medium. Many felt that he was too harsh in his judgment of Blavatsky. In 1887, he accepted the position of executive secretary of the American branch of the SPR and immediately began investigating Piper, hiring a detective agency to follow her every move. Until his death eighteen years later, he observed hundreds of sittings with Piper and was eventually convinced of her ability. "…I cannot profess to have any doubt but that the chief communicators are veritably the personalities that they claim to be, that they have survived the change we call death, and that they have directly communicated with us whom we call living, through Mrs. Piper's entranced organism," Hodgson reported (Baird 1949).

Among many things observed by Hodgson was Phinuit speaking through Piper's entranced organism at the same time her hand was writing freely and rapidly on other subjects while purportedly being controlled by another spirit. Hodgson reported that when the hand was writing independently of Phinuit's speech, the sense of hearing for the "hand-control" appeared to be in the hand, whereas Phinuit apparently always heard through the ordinary channel. On at least one occasion, Phinuit was speaking on one subject while both hands were writing on different subjects, each hand controlled by different spirits; i.e., three spirits communicating at the same time. Hodgson noted that the left hand was much slower than the right hand in recording information, apparently because Piper's organism was not accustomed to using it for that purpose.

Dr. Richard Hodgson.

None of the many investigators who observed Piper considered her a fraud, but there were some who questioned whether Dr. Phinuit had ever lived. The early theory held by almost all the researchers was that he was some kind of "secondary personality" buried away in Piper's subconscious. While he gave his name as Jean Phinuit Sclivelle to Hodgson and said that he had married Marie Latimer, he told Lodge that his name was John Phinuit Schelevelle or Clavelle and that his wife's name was Mary. He told both of them that he had studied medicine at "Metz" in Germany. However, no record of his name could be found. There were other strange inconsistencies, including his inability to speak French to some sitters fluent in French. Although Piper knew no French, Phinuit was able to speak French to several sitters, including J. Rogers Rich. The fact that he wasn't sure about the year of his birth or death also went to his credibility, although other communicating spirits have said they lose a sense of time in the spirit world and are unable to remember certain details about their earthly lives.

But the secondary personality theory failed to explain the hundreds of known deceased personalities communicating through Piper. And if that secondary personality, whatever that is, was somehow reading the minds of the sitters, the researchers wondered how can such things as Rich's deceased sister, whom he knew nothing about, be explained?

What seems to have swayed most of the researchers away from the secondary personality theory is the fact that beginning in 1894, Phinuit started turning over his "control" function to others in the spirit world—people whose existence could be verified. One of the later controls was Hodgson himself, who began communicating through Piper shortly after his death in 1905. If Phinuit's successors could be confirmed as having been alive in the flesh at one time, then why not Phinuit?

Eight

A Change of Controls for Mrs. Piper

…I had a wonderful sitting with Mrs. Piper. As you know, I have been a Laodicean toward her heretofore. But that she is no fraud, and that she is the greatest marvel I have ever met I am now wholly convinced.

—Professor Herbert Nichols (in a letter to William James)

Soon after Dr. Richard Hodgson moved to the United States from England and began investigating the mediumship of Leonora Piper he met George Pellew, an associate of the American Society for Psychical Research (ASPR), of which Hodgson served as executive secretary. A member of a prominent New York family and a Harvard graduate with a law degree, Pellew was a writer and poet. He authored at least six books, including biographies of statesmen John Jay and Henry Addington and one on poetry. In February 1892, at the age of thirty-two, Pellew died after a fall from a horse.

Hodgson later recalled having had several long philosophical discussions about the possibility of a "future life" with Pellew, who told him that he could not conceive of an afterlife. However, he was open-minded on the subject and told Hodgson that if he should die before Hodgson and found himself "still existing," he would attempt to let Hodgson know.

On March 22, 1892, a little over a month after Pellew's death, Hodgson arranged a sitting for John Hart, a friend of Pellew, with Piper. Pellew's actual name was not made public until many years later and Hodgson gave him the pseudonym "George Pelham." Early in the sitting, Phinuit, Piper's primary spirit control, announced that "George" was there. Phinuit gave Pellew's real name and the names of several close friends, including the sitter. To give assurance that it was actually him communicating through Phinuit, Pellew told Hart that the pair of studs he was wearing were once his and were given to Hart by his (Pellew's) parents, which Hart confirmed as true. Pellew then (again, Phinuit relaying the messages through the entranced medium) mentioned some mutual friends, Jim and Mary Howard, and asked Hart if he could get them to attend a sitting. He also brought up a discussion he had had with Katharine, the Howards' fifteen-year-old daughter, about God, space, and eternity. As neither Hart nor Hodgson, who was also in attendance and taking notes, was aware of any such discussion with Katharine, this information, later verified as fact, certainly fell outside the scope of telepathy, a dominant theory then.

Hodgson recorded that many personal references were made by Pellew and that Hart was very impressed, mentioning that various words of greetings and speech mannerisms were very characteristic of Pellew, even though then relayed through Phinuit.

Some three weeks later, Jim and Mary Howard had a sitting with Piper. Apparently, they did not believe in such things, but were so bewildered by Hart's account of his sitting that they decided to attend. As was the procedure, Hodgson did not tell Piper their names or give her any clue as to their connection with Pellew. Yet, Pellew communicated. However, rather than Phinuit speaking through Piper and relaying messages from Pellew, Pellew took over Piper's body and spoke directly to his friends. "Jim is that you?" Hodgson recorded Pellew's initial greeting. "Speak to me quick. I am not dead. Don't think me dead. I'm awfully glad to see you. Can't you see me?

Don't you hear me? Give my love to my father and tell him I want to see him. I am happy here, and more so since I can communicate with you. I pity those people who can't speak…" (Holt 1914).

Pellew went on to tell his friends that he was very limited in what he could do as he had just "awakened to the reality of life after death," adding that he was greatly surprised as he did not believe in a future life. He told them it was all darkness at first and that he was puzzled and confused. He said that he could see Jim, but that his voice sounded like a big bass drum. Jim Howard asked Pellew if he was surprised to find himself still living. "Perfectly so," Pellew responded. "Greatly surprised. I did not believe in a future life. It was beyond my reasoning powers. Now it is as clear to me as daylight. We have an astral facsimile of the material body" (Holt 1914).

At a later sitting, the Howards brought their daughter, Katharine. Pellew came through and asked Katharine about her violin lessons, commenting (apparently jesting) that her playing was "horrible." Not realizing the humor in it, Mary Howard spoke up to defend her daughter's music, but Pellew then explained that he mentioned it because that is what he used to do when in the flesh. It was intended as verification of his identity. Phinuit then broke in and took back control from Pellew, commenting that Pellew had bypassed him by mistake and that he would act as the go-between the remainder of the session. Phinuit began speaking fluent French to Katharine, who had lived in France and knew the language. Someone known to Mary Howard as Madame Elisa then interrupted, speaking in Italian. Mary Howard responded in Italian. (It should be kept in mind that Piper did not know French or Italian.)

However, there was some confusion on Pellew's part in responding to various questions put to him by Howard. Pellew explained that he was somewhat "dull" in his new sphere and that his memory was not much different than when he was on the earth plane; thing in a moment. He went on to say that he had lost all sense of time in his new environment. But he was determined to make his identity clear. "Hodgson, I mean, and Jim, I want you both to feel I am no secondary personality of the medium's [sic]," he told them, adding that he lives, thinks, sees, hears, knows, and feels just as clearly as when he was in the material life. "…but it is not so easy to explain it to you as you would naturally suppose, especially when the thoughts have to be expressed through substance materially" (Holt 1914).

Pellew further discussed the problems of communicating, pointing out that there is a conflict between the spiritual ego, or mind, of the communicating spirit and the material mind or ego of the medium that is very difficult to overcome. He explained that when Piper went into trance, her ego left the body, just as when a person is sleeping, and although her brain is left empty, it is very difficult for the communicating spirit to control it. He also mentioned that it was much easier to communicate with someone in "sympathy" with him; e.g., a friend or relative, than it was to communicate with a skeptical researcher. He said that to those in his sphere, we humans are "sleeping" in the material world; we are in what is to them a "dream-life." For them to communicate with us, they have to enter this sleep state, which adds to the confusion.

Phinuit added to Pellew's comments about the difficulty of seeing things, likening it to looking through a keyhole into a room and trying to describe what the people were doing in the other room as they passed back and forth through the room.

At a later sitting, when the Howards were not present, Hodgson asked Pellew if he could visit the Howards home and report back by the end of the sitting what they were doing. Toward the end of the sitting, Pellew interrupted Phinuit to give his report. He found only Mrs. Howard at home and reported on her writing letters to his (Pellew's) mother as well as somebody named Tyson. He also saw her handling a book he (Pellew) had written and wondering if he (Pellew) was around at the time. Several other routine tasks were reported. When Hodgson checked with Mrs. Howard to see if the report was true, she confirmed that it was accurate, except that it all happened on the previous day, not the day of the sitting. Hodgson didn't know what to make of that, but he surmised that the agent (Mrs. Howard) in such an experiment had to be thinking of the subject (Pellew) for it to be successful. Pellew, who had an obscure perception of the physical world, including time, had somehow tapped into her subliminal consciousness for the most recent activities in which he was emotionally on her mind.

As a further test of telepathy, Mrs. Howard brought three pictures to a sitting and asked Pellew to identify them. Pellew correctly identified the first picture as the Howards summer home. He correctly identified a second picture as a country place where they had stayed, recalling a little brick henhouse which was not in the picture. Mrs. Howard confirmed the accuracy of this report and then showed a third picture, which Pellew could not identify. In fact, Pellew had never seen it. Had Piper been reading Howard's mind she should have been able to identify it, unless, of course, she could also read Howard's mind relative to the test, and her subconscious was aware and devious enough to know that it was more important to show ignorance than it was to identify the location in the picture.

Over time it became evident that Pellew had learned to manage the medium's organism without Phinuit's assistance. Thus, he became a "control" himself. It was not until Pellew began using her organism that Piper fully developed the ability of automatic writing.

Until Pellew began communicating, Hodgson subscribed to the secondary personality and telepathy theories. That is, Phinuit, her control, was a fragmented personality buried away in her subconscious and this fragmented personality could, unknown to Piper's primary personality, read the minds of the sitters. When information was transmitted that was unknown to the sitter, that theory began to fall apart. But, the spirit theory was apparently too simplistic for intelligent researchers to accept, and so a theory called "teloteropathy" developed. This theory held that it is possible to pick up thoughts from a person anywhere in the world. It was later expanded to suggest that there is some kind of cosmic reservoir where every thought or utterance ever made is recorded. It is now generally referred to as "superpsi" or "super-ESP."

But the communication with Pellew caused Hodgson to abandon all other theories in favor of the spirit one. While the existence of Phinuit could not be verified, there was no doubt that Pellew had lived in the flesh. Moreover, there was too much individuality, too much purpose and persistence, expressed by Pellew to attribute it to telepathy of a limited or expanded nature. It was one thing for a medium to tap into another mind or cosmic reservoir for information, quite another for that other mind or reservoir to come back with the fullness of a personality rather than just fragmentary bits of information.

Hodgson noted that when someone Pellew had known when he was alive happened to be sitting, he (Pellew) would greet him or her by name. When someone unknown to him was sitting, he didn't address the person by name. The non-recognition went against any telepathy theory. "There are thirty cases of true recognition out of at least one hundred and fifty persons who have had sittings with Mrs. Piper since the first appearance of G.P. (George Pellew), and no case of false recognition," Hodgson reported. "The continual manifestation of this personality—so different from Phinuit or other communicators—with its own reservoir of memories, with its swift appreciation of any reference to friends of G.P., with its 'give and take' in little incidental conversations with myself, has helped largely in producing a conviction of the actual presence of the G.P. personality, which it would be quite impossible to impart by any mere enumeration of the verifiable statements" (Holt 1914).

Gradually, Pellew took over from Phinuit as Piper's primary control and most of the information communicated came by way of automatic writing rather than through Piper's voice. Phinuit continued as a secondary control and would sometimes complain that Pellew was too domineering. "I never saw the like of that fellow George," Phinuit grumbled to Hodgson. "There's another here trying to say something but he gave no chance at all. When he gets hold he keeps hold I tell you Hodgson" (Holt 1914).

At a sitting on June 17, 1895, Hodgson asked Pellew what Phinuit was doing when he (Pellew) was the only one using Piper's body. Pellew replied that Phinuit was holding back "a million others" from interrupting him. In one of twenty-six sittings by Professor William R. Newbold of the University of Pennsylvania, Phinuit was talking to Newbold while Pellew was writing on behalf of another communicating spirit. Several times, Newbold heard Phinuit tell someone not to be in a hurry, that there was plenty of time. Newbold thought he was talking to him and asked Phinuit what he meant. Phinuit explained that he was talking to a young man in spirit who was in a great hurry to begin communicating. When the young man finally got through, he was recognized as Hodgson's recently deceased brother. However, he was apparently still "awakening" on the other side and made very little sense.

In another case, one spirit interrupted a communication by another spirit, prompting Hodgson to become upset and speak roughly to her. Phinuit told Hodgson that the woman called him a "brute" and went away with very hurt feelings. He added that they (Pellew and Phinuit) were trying to coax her to come back, but she refused.

Beginning in 1895, the quality of the messages began to deteriorate and there were indications that devious earthbound spirits were able to control Piper's organism. Deceased writers Sir Walter Scott and George Eliot supposedly communicated directly through Piper's hand, but the nature of the communication suggested impostors.

Pellew and Phinuit gradually gave way to "Rector" of the Imperator band. Rector told them that Piper's organism was weakening and needed a rest. While Rector and the band of forty-nine continued to use Piper's organism, it was with more care than Pellew and Phinuit could provide. Rector said they were substituting a "softer melody" for the rough, inharmonious and uncultivated dialect, referring primarily to Phinuit. While not "earth earthy," Rector said that Phinuit was too bound by the attractions of earthly minds. Phinuit made his last appearance on January 26, 1896. It was later reported that he had advanced and gone on to other work.

On June 8, 1897, Pellew warned Hodgson not to accept anything further as coming from him, implying that it might be an earthbound spirit posing as him. He added that he might not have the pleasure of seeing him for a long time. Rector cautioned Hodgson not to rely too much on Pellew as he was "too far away," i.e., too advanced, to be effective. "His spirit is pure, his mind sincere, his whole life here is one of honor and one to be respected by us all," Rector wrote through Piper's hand. "Yet, we would speak the truth and say his work in your field is done" (Holt 1914). However, Pellew apparently continued as an assistant to Rector for a number of years, at least until 1904.

Nine

Boston Mayor Communicates through Mrs. Piper

Practically I should be willing now to stake as much money on Mrs. Piper's honesty as on that of anyone I know, and I am quite satisfied to leave my reputation for wisdom or folly, so far as human nature is concerned, to stand or fall by this declaration.

—Professor William James

When he was alive, Augustus P. Martin, mayor of the city of Boston during the early 1880s, courteously smiled and shrugged when Anne Manning Robbins, his secretary, told him about her sittings with the renowned Boston trance medium Leonora Piper, and how she had communicated with deceased friends and relatives through Piper. While Martin apparently didn't really approve of her "dabbling in the occult," he was too much of a gentleman to criticize her.

In her 1909 book, *Both Sides of the Veil,* Robbins recalled Martin as a man of "dignity, sweetness and light." She recorded that he listened patiently to the complaint of the poorest petitioner for justice and was like an old

Roman patrician might have been, a father to all young people who worked for him. "The geniality of his nature and the kindly courtesy of his manner made themselves felt like sunlight in the quarters which he occupied daily, and during all my experience in office life I have never known a man more loved by other men than was he," Manning wrote (Robbins 1909). Known as the "General," after Massachusetts Governor John Long commissioned him an honorary brigadier general because of his distinguished service during the Civil War, especially at the Battle of Gettysburg, Martin served as Boston police commissioner and then as water commissioner after his term as mayor.

At a sitting with Piper on January 17, 1900, Imperator, Piper's primary spirit control at that time, communicated to Robbins via Piper's entranced body, that she and Martin would write a book together. When Robbins asked Imperator what it would be about, he replied: "It is concerning the natural things in life and many different conditions of thy life, which will be put together in a form of philosophy. It will be so in spite of anything which thou mayst think to the contrary" (Robbins 1909).

While Robbins, a graduate of Mount Holyoke College, was a competent writer and worked well with Martin, she could not imagine the two of them collaborating on a book of any kind. At a later sitting, she told Imperator that she had no desire to write a book. "Friend, to write a book, it is thy doom or duty, one and both combined," Imperator replied (Robbins 1909).

After Martin's death on March 13, 1902, Robbins wrote off the prediction as "failed prophecy." But Robbins had had too many meaningful and evidential sittings with Piper to discount everything because of that. She still trusted in Imperator and Rector, who had replaced Dr. Phinuit and George Pellew as Piper's spirit controls in 1897, some twelve years after Robbins's first sitting with Piper. The *modus operandi* was for Piper to go into a trance and then for either Imperator or Rector to take over her body and communicate by means of automatic writing. Imperator, who was said to be a very high spirit, would communicate only when he had some profound

Augustus P. Martin, Mayor of Boston.

wisdom to relate. When deceased relatives and friends wanted to communicate with the sitter, Rector would take over and relay the messages from the various spirits through Piper's hand. Earlier, under the Phinuit regime, messages came from Piper's mouth, but the writing method proved to be more effective.

Because of her stenographic ability, Robbins was asked by Dr. Richard Hodgson, the chief investigator of the Piper phenomena, to assist him at times, keeping a record of the questions put to the communicating spirits by sitters before Piper's hand gave the answers. On May 21, 1903, Piper was coming out of trance and still in a dazed condition when Robbins heard her, or her control, mutter something about General Martin coming soon to speak. However, it wasn't until December 23 that year, some 21 months after his passing, that Martin actually began to communicate. "I want to know if you don't think we could manage to write a book?" Martin communicated through Piper, clearly and strongly, adding that he had had this on his mind ever since making the transition to his new world (Robbins 1909). When Robbins asked him why he had waited two years to communicate, he explained that he was "grappling" and that it took him that long for his spirit to fully awaken and adapt.

Over the next six years, Martin communicated with Robbins in a number of sittings, often discussing life on his side of the veil and his new philosophy resulting from it. "I am quite the man that I was, only my ideas are all changed," Martin said through Rector. "They are more now I think in harmony with your own…But, oh, why was I so blind? It was because of the thickness, the thickness of the flesh" (Robbins 1909).

Robbins asked Martin where he was and if he could see her and what she was doing. Martin replied that he was standing next to Piper with his hand on her shoulder. He could see Piper's hand writing something and could also see Robbins's hand writing. However, he didn't fully comprehend what was going on with all the writing. Robbins explained to him that his thoughts were coming out through Piper's hand. Martin said that "they" (apparently Rector and other assistants of Imperator's) had been giving him instructions for months and months of earth time on how to communicate, but the process was very confusing and it was still being hammered into him.

Robbins asked Martin if he could remember what happened immediately after his death in the physical. "When I first passed out my mind was cloudy, rather confused," he responded. "I felt as though I was going into space, did not know where, drifting as it were, for a few hours—that was all—and then I felt as though a strong hand grasped me and said to me: 'It is all right, it is over.' And I said, 'What is over?' I could not seem to understand what it all meant, and after a little while, perhaps an hour, possibly an hour or two, I saw, oh, such a light! You cannot imagine it, cannot conceive what it is like" (Robbins 1909).

The guide who greeted Martin explained to him that he was now in the "real life." Although still confused, Martin recalled then being welcomed by friends and relatives. "Why, I felt as though I should be enveloped by them, the delight was so great, but when I tried to call them by name I was at a loss to do so," he related. "They had to tell me who they were. I knew their faces, not one failed me." When Martin tried to speak, he found that it was by thought transference rather than by vocal cords. "There was a perfect communion between us" (Robbins 1909). He also recalled observing his own funeral and feeling relieved that he had been released from the imprisoning body.

"I have been advancing and going on, and I have seen everybody I ever knew, and I have had the happiest time you could imagine," Martin continued, going on to say that after his initial orientation he was taken to an "actual mansion". (Robbins, 1909) It had beautiful flowers around it and there was an orchestra there to welcome him with beautiful music. "Now you are not living in the real life," Martin told Robbins, realizing that it is hard for those incarnate to understand how there can be seemingly material things in the spirit world. "You are living in a dream, as it were. When you awaken from the dream you will live in the eternal life" (Robbins 1909). He went on to explain that life on his side of the veil is not a "facsimile" of earthly life; rather, it is the other way around. Everything in the earth life is an imitation of the real life. He referred to earthly life as a "miserable shadow" of what life on that side is really like.

During one sitting, Martin said that he was getting too weak to remain. Robbins mentioned that that they had been communicating for nearly an hour. Martin replied that he no longer had any concept of how long an hour was, but that he could not use the "light" (Piper's organism) any longer as it was losing strength. After bidding farewell, Rector offered a few words, commenting that Martin "has a very earnest desire to work for God and humanity" (Robbins 1909).

At a sitting on May 24, 1904, Martin told Robbins that he was frequently standing by her side when she didn't realize it. He added that when she was working he sometimes dictated thoughts to her and was surprised to see how clearly she registered them, noting that he could sense her surprise when she stopped to give some thought at to what she had just recorded. He related that as he had progressed in the spiritual world, he had forgotten the names of various people and places, but that the vital ones, those for which he had "real spiritual sympathies" remained with him. He recalled a person named "Hanscom" who was discharged from the police force due to some disagreement. Martin said he didn't really appreciate Hanscom's point of view then, but that he was now able to "see his principles" and better understand Hanscom's broad outlook and ideas of reform. He asked Robbins to tell Hanscom that he now appreciated his efforts if she could do it in such a way that Hanscom would not think her crazy.

When Robbins asked Martin what he did with his time, he replied that his "time" was "completely filled." He explained that he was actively engaged in welcoming and instructing spirits who had just passed over from the earth life, remaining with them until they were fully conscious. Some were taken to another sphere, but he was able to work with those who remained on his level. He also visited with friends, played musical instruments, wrote, lectured, enjoyed his garden, and attended lectures and concerts of all kinds. "It is a perfect life," he went on. "And in order to live this perfect life you have got to live that imperfect life, and the more you undertake to prepare for this life the less you have to go through when you pass to it and the clearer your thoughts become when you enter it" (Robbins 1909). But Martin cautioned Robbins not to be in a big hurry to quit this life, stating that every person must live out his or her allotted time, and that a person who takes his life intentionally is set back in development and unfolding.

Martin told Robbins that even though she couldn't remember it when awake, her spirit went out upon her ethereal cord when she was asleep, during which time she often visited and talked with him. He further said that he had never seen God and never expected to, pointing out that God rules us all and reigns over us all, and that we are a branch of Him.

Martin also told Robbins that George Pellew had helped him quite a bit in learning how to communicate, although Pellew had advanced to the seventh sphere, what people on earth speak of as heaven, and therefore quite distant from earthly conditions. Robbins then asked Martin what sphere he was in, to which he replied, the third. "We advance until we feel that we have perfected ourselves according to God's will and idea, and then we have satisfied ourselves, and not until we have," he explained, going on to say that the Bible passage, "In my Father's house there are many mansions," has a literal meaning (Robbins 1909).

Robbins asked Martin if a spirit on one of the lower spheres or planes could see and talk with him. Martin replied that it was possible if the spirit had a great desire to do so and complied with certain conditions through which he must pass. As for beings on higher realms, they appeared as flickering rays with faces, but those on Martin's realm did not usually come in close proximity with them because they were too progressed.

"I have learned so much about this beautiful life and realize the truth and reality of it by having the actual experience, that the world should through your hand and brain be made cognizant in part of the unfoldment, of the true development of the soul after it leaves its environment," Martin said. "That it is an active consciousness, that it is in the state of higher development, that it is able to reach the physical plane and act through voices as your own, we would say, to give expression and utterance to the truth and reality of in part what this life contains" (Robbins 1909).

His biggest regret, Martin offered, was not learning more about it when he was alive as this hindered his progress once he made his transition to the other side of the veil.

Ten

Dr. Hodgson Returns through Mrs. Piper

Well if I am not Hodgson, he never lived.

—(the discarnate) **Richard Hodgson**

In 1884, while teaching philosophy at Cambridge and legal studies at University Extension, Richard Hodgson was recruited by the Society for Psychical Research (SPR) to investigate mediums. He turned in unfavorable reports on several mediums, including Madame Blavatsky. Many felt that he was too quick to judge and too harsh. It appeared that he was out to debunk all mediums. After moving to the United States in 1887 and investigating the mediumship of Leonora Piper of Boston, he came to believe in the authenticity of her gift.

As the only full-time employee of the American branch of the SPR (ASPR), Hodgson had hundreds of sittings with Piper between 1887 and his death on December 20, 1905, when, at age fifty, he had a heart attack while playing handball. Eight days after his death, Miss Theodate Pope, who had known Hodgson, was having a sitting with Piper. Rector, Piper's spirit control, was using her organism and writing something when the hand dropped the pencil and started shaking. When the hand steadied itself, it wrote the letter "H," after which the point of the pencil was broken. When a new pencil was placed in Piper's hand, it wrote "Hodgson." It started to write something else, but only rapid scrawls followed.

Rector then took back control of the medium and explained that Hodgson was there, but that he was too "choked" to write. It wasn't until another sitting by Pope five days later that Hodgson communicated again, beginning with a poem. However, he added that he felt confused and could write no more. At a third sitting, on January 8, 1906, Hodgson came again and explained that it was extremely difficult for him to communicate, suggesting that he had not yet awakened enough or that he had not yet learned how to handle the "mechanism" (Piper's body).

On January 23, 1906, Mrs. William James, wife of the renowned Harvard professor, and William James, Jr. sat with Piper. Hodgson used Piper's voice mechanism and said: "Why, there's Billy! Is that Mrs. James and Billy? God bless you! Well, well, this is good! (laughs) I am in the witness box. (laughs) I have found my way, I am here, have patience with me…Where's William?…I am not strong, but have patience with me…I will tell you all…" (Holt 1914).

Hodgson went on to say that he had seen Frederic Myers (pioneering psychical researcher who died in 1901) and wanted Sir Oliver Lodge (another psychical researcher, still alive) to know everything. He asked James Jr. about his swimming and fishing, two activities they had enjoyed together. He also asked James Jr. if he could give George Dorr, who was handling some of his affairs, instructions about his (Hodgson's) private papers. There was much other evidential information indicating that it was indeed Hodgson communicating. Hodgson closed with a comment saying that communication was much more difficult than he had anticipated while alive and that he now understood why Myers communicated so little.

When a Mrs. Lyman had a sitting with Piper, Hodgson brought up a ring that she had given him for his fiftieth birthday. He said he wanted it to go back to her, but he did not know what happened to it. He speculated that the undertaker took it and then that the locker room attendant at the club where he died might have it. However, it was later found in his waistcoat at Dorr's home. On May 2, 1906, Hodgson told the sitter, John Piddington, who was assisting George Dorr in handling his affairs, that he did not want anyone to read the letters he had saved from a lady friend. Hodgson gave "Huldah" as the name of his friend. On May 14, Piddington reported back to Hodgson that no such letters could be found among his belongings. Hodgson replied that he may have destroyed them and forgotten it. On June 5, Mrs. James and Dorr sat with Piper and asked Hodgson about his love interest. Hodgson said that he had once proposed marriage to her, but she had refused. He gave the full name as Ella Huldah Densmore. William James later contacted Densmore to confirm the story, as this was something unknown to any of Hodgson's friends and seemingly outside the scope of normal telepathy. He found out that her middle name was Hannah, not Huldah, but she verified that Hodgson had once proposed marriage to her and that they had exchanged letters.

As the American branch of the SPR was often short of funds, Hodgson did not always receive his full salary. A wealthy friend sometimes donated money to make up the deficit. However, it was donated through one of the ASPR officers with the understanding that Hodgson not know where the money came from, as the friend did not want Hodgson to in any way feel obligated to him. When that friend had a sitting with Piper, Hodgson communicated and thanked him for his support.

Over the next seven or eight months, many people who had known Hodgson had sittings with Piper. The discarnate Hodgson did his best to provide bits of information that would allow them to recognize that he was communicating, and that it was not all some mind-reading game. But as communicating spirits had indicated to Hodgson when he was alive and studying Piper, it was not all that easy to get information through. The discarnate Hodgson said that it was very difficult to remember names and that some earthly memories came and went. Even when he was alive, he was poor with names and recollections. The fact that he was now operating in a different realm did not mean that he could remember them any better. Moreover, there were difficulties in communicating various things through the medium's organism.

"I find now difficulties such as a blind man would experience in trying to find his hat," Hodgson told Professor William Newbold in a July 23, 1906, sitting. "And I am not wholly conscious of my own utterances because they come out automatically, impressed upon the machine (Piper's body)…I impress my thoughts on the machine which registers them at random, and which are at times doubtless difficult to understand. I understand so much better the modus operandi than I did when I was in your world" (Holt 1914).

When Newbold asked Hodgson if he could see him, Hodgson replied that he could but that he could feel his presence better. He added that he stood behind Newbold and William James as they were discussing him (Hodgson) the prior week and could hear their conversation. He recalled James saying that he (Hodgson) was very "secretive and careful." Newbold said he did not recall that comment. "I tell you, Billy, he said so," Hodgson exclaimed (Holt 1914). James later confirmed that he did make such a statement.

When Dr. James Hyslop, another renowned psychical researcher of that era, sat with Piper, Hodgson asked him if he remembered a conversation when he (Hodgson) said that if he died first and were able to communicate he would talk with the fervor of a southern preacher. Hyslop said he did not remember any such conversation. Hodgson then recalled that it was William James with whom he had had the conversation. Hyslop later contacted James to see if such a statement had been made. James confirmed it, although his recollection was that he made the statement to Hodgson.

Except for the vocal greeting to Mrs. James and her son, the communication from Hodgson came through Piper's hand in writing. Rector would often relay the messages from Hodgson, but there were times when Rector stepped aside and allowed Hodgson to take control. James asked Hodgson why it was necessary for Rector to assist him in the communication so often. Hodg-

Dr. James Hyslop.

son explained that Rector better understood the "management of the light."

When James chided Hodgson on his handwriting, commenting that it was getting worse, Hodgson asked James if he recalled a time that he (Hodgson) wrote to him in London, but James found his handwriting so "detestable" that he had to ask his daughter, Margaret, to read it. James could not clearly remember it, but his daughter remembered it perfectly.

According to James, who had a number of sittings with Piper when Hodgson communicated, there was a lively feeling that the personality communicating, whether Rector or Hodgson, understood the whole situation. Hodgson talked about certain records of the ASPR not being made public, about the disposition of his books and other property, about the future of the ASPR, and about a certain individual who was unduly interfering with the organization. "One who takes part in a good sitting has usually a far more lively sense, both of the reality and of the importance of the communication, than one who merely reads the record," James wrote. "Active relations with a thing are required to bring the reality of it home to us, and in a trance-talk the sitter actively cooperates" (Holt 1914).

And yet, James struggled with accepting the spirit hypothesis over the secondary personality, telepathy, and teloteropathy (the latter being telepathy from a distance) hypotheses. Hodgson had the same struggle until George Pellew began communicating through Piper (Holt 1914). There was simply too much personality, too much emotion, too much persistence in the communication for Hodgson to cling to the mind-reading theory, where one would expect fragmentary bits of information, not dramatic dialogue. As indicated by his reports to the ASPR, James, who apparently found the spirit hypothesis either too simplistic or too complex, gradually came to believe there might be something to it.

"If your imagination is incapable of conceiving the spirit hypothesis at all, you will just proclaim it 'impossible' and thus confess yourself incompetent to discuss the alternative seriously," James wrote. "I myself can perfectly well imagine spirit-agency, and I find my mind vacillating about it curiously" (Holt 1914).

While mind-reading might have explained Hodgson's comment about fishing and swimming to James Jr., it did not explain how Piper's secondary personality turned fragmentary bits of information extracted from the conscious or subconscious of James Jr. into questions and discussions. It did not explain the discussion that Hodgson had concerning ASPR affairs, unless one accepts the possibility that a secondary personality can rapidly process information and then turn it into a dialogue, sometimes dramatically. Even if a secondary personality knew about Dorr handling Hodgson's affairs, how could "it" know what was in those papers? What cosmic computer might the secondary personality have tapped into in coming up with "Huldah" and the marriage proposal to her? If there is some cosmic computer in the ethers, why couldn't the secondary personality of Piper get the name straight? Why couldn't the secondary personality get other names that were clearly in the minds of the sitters? Can a secondary personality have a will to deceive? These were all questions that James pondered, certain, however, that Mrs. Piper's non-trance personality was totally honest and sincere.

"If you can give up to it, William, and feel the influence of it and the reality of it, it will take away the sting of death," Hodgson advised James concerning his skepticism, adding that James expected too much from him, as if he should be able to communicate as effectively and coherently as he could in the body (Holt 1914).

In November 1906, Piper returned to England to be further tested by Sir Oliver Lodge, the renowned physicist and psychical researcher. Lodge noted that when he first sat with Piper in 1889, communication was almost always with the voice and any writing was brief and occasional. Now, seventeen years later, it was just the opposite, almost everything in writing and the voice employed only under exceptional circumstances. In 1889, Piper sat upright with head bowed and eyes closed. In 1906, her head reclined on a cushion with her face turned away as her right hand alone was active. "The dramatic activity of the hand was very remarkable," Lodge wrote. "It was full of intelligence, and could be described as more like an intelligent person than a hand. It sometimes turned to the sitter, when it wanted to be spoken to by him, but for the most part, when not writing, it turned itself away from the sitter, as if receiving communications from outside, which it then proceeded to write down, going back to space, i.e., directing itself to a part of the room where nobody was—for further information and supplementary intelligence, as necessity arose" (Lodge 1909).

Lodge described a typical sitting: Piper would enter the room at a designated time, seat herself in the chair in front of the pillows, after which the experimenter (usually Lodge) sat near the table on which Piper's right hand would write. The sitter would usually not enter the room until Piper was in the trance state. It usually took about five minutes for her to enter trance, at which time her head dropped onto her hands on the pillows and turned itself to the left. Her right hand would then disengage itself and fall on the table near the writing materials. After about 30 seconds, the hand would "wake up," slowly rise, make the sign of the cross in the air, and indicate that it was ready to write. Lodge would then give the hand a pencil, placing it between the fore and middle fingers. It would at once be grasped and writing began. First, a cross would be drawn and then the word "Hail" was written, after which followed words of salutation and the signature "R," for Rector. It was up to the experimenter to change the paper when a page was complete. The hand seemed to know when to pause, but often became impatient if the experimenter was too slow in replacing the paper.

Lodge further observed that in 1889, when Phinuit was controlling Piper, going into trance always appeared a very painful process, involving much contortion and even a pulling of her hair. However, under Rector's control, Piper achieved the trance state much more serenely and the return to consciousness was much easier and natural than in the Phinuit days. In 1889, Piper would often be tested twice a day, but Rector would now permit only about every other day and then for a two-hour limit. As she emerged from the trance state, Piper would remain somewhat dazed for about thirty minutes, often mumbling, until her eyes brightened and she recognized people in the room.

Hodgson appeared a number of times in Piper's English sittings, but pretty much stayed in the background so that others could communicate with familiar sitters.

Gladys Osborne Leonard.

Part III

Chapters 11–14

The Mediumship of Gladys Osborne Leonard, England's "White Crow"

A great medium is a rare phenomenon, rarer than a great painter or piano virtuoso. The world has produced only a few mediums whose powers were so outstanding that they could be called great. Gladys Osborne Leonard is one of these.

— **Susy Smith**, American journalist and author

Eleven

Raymond Returns from the Battlefield

I am as convinced of continued existence on the other side of death, as I am of existence here.

—Sir Oliver Lodge

On September 14, 1915, Second Lieutenant Raymond Lodge, the youngest son of Sir Oliver Lodge, a renowned British physicist and educator, was killed in action in Flanders. Eleven days later, on September 25, a message was received for Sir Oliver from Raymond: "Tell father I have met some friends of his" (Lodge 1916).

The message was given to Lady Lodge, Sir Oliver's wife, at a sitting with Gladys Osborne Leonard, then a relatively unknown medium. Lady Lodge had gone to Mrs. Leonard as a complete stranger, not giving her name. Raymond's comment about his father's friends was preceded with some discourse with his mother in which Lady Lodge sought to verify that it was, in fact, her son communicating. After the comment about Sir Oliver's friends, Lady Lodge asked if the spirit purporting to be her son could give any names. "Yes, Myers," was the reply (Lodge 1916).

Upon being told of this startling message, Sir Oliver arranged a sitting with Leonard two days later. He also went to her house as a complete stranger after an appointment had been made by a friend. Raymond then communicated directly with his father. Feda, Leonard's spirit control, who would take over the vocal cords of the entranced medium, told Sir Oliver that Raymond said he was confused at first and didn't know where he was, but he had many friends helping him adjust to his new environment on the "other side." Among them was his father's old friend, Frederic W. H. Myers, who had crossed over in 1901. "I feel I have got two fathers now," Raymond communicated. "I don't feel I have lost one and got another; I have got both. I have got my old one, and another too—a *pro tem.* father" (Lodge 1916).

Later on the same day that Sir Oliver had a sitting with Leonard, Lady Lodge sat with Alfred Vout Peters, another London medium to whom she went anonymously. Here also, Raymond communicated, again referring to "Myers." Sir Oliver then went for his own sitting with Peters. "After the grief there was a glimmering of hope, because he realized he could get back to you," Moonstone, Peters's spirit control, communicated from Raymond. "And because his grandmother came to him. Then, he says, other people. Myerse—Myerse, it sounds like—do you know what he means?—came to him, and then he knew he could get back. He knew" (Lodge 1916).

The fuller story began more than 30 years earlier when Lodge became interested in the subject of mental telepathy, then called thought-transference. Like so many other scientists caught up in the wake of Darwinism, Lodge had become a materialist, not believing in anything spiritual. However, he remained open-minded on the subject and was intrigued by the idea that one person could read another's mind, something he had observed around 1883 in a stage performer called Irving Bishop. "The verification of the fact of telepathy, indicating obscurely a kind of dislocation between mind and body, was undoubtedly impressive, so that it began to seem probable, especially under Myers's tuition, that the two –mind and body—were not inseparably connected, as I had been led by my previous studies under Clifford, Tyndall, and Huxley to believe they were," Lodge, who spent most

Raymond Lodge.

of his career as principal of University College in Liverpool, wrote in his autobiography (Lodge 1932).

Myers, a classics scholar and lecturer at Cambridge University, was one of the founders of the Society for Psychical Research (SPR), organized in London in 1882. Although not educated as a psychologist, Myers has been credited with developing a systematic conception of the subliminal self as well as a theory holding that telepathy is one of the basic laws of life. In fact, it was Myers who coined the term "telepathy."

After Lodge joined the SPR around 1885, he and Myers became good friends. It was Myers, Lodge explained, who broke down his skepticism and showed him the reasonableness of the survival hypothesis, i.e., life after death. "He it was who put evidence in my way such as gradually convinced me of the truth of the doctrine," Lodge wrote (Lodge 1932).

Lodge's best early evidence came from the mediumship of Leonora Piper. It was Lodge's first experience with a trance medium and he was very much impressed, especially when his Aunt Anne, who was very close to him when he was growing up, communicated in a voice that Lodge so well remembered, and reminded him of her promise to come back if she could.

On August 8, 1915, some five weeks before Raymond Lodge was killed in action, Anne Manning Robbins was having a sitting with Mrs. Piper in New Hampshire when a somewhat cryptic message came from Myers for Sir Oliver. Myers told Lodge that he (Lodge) should take the part of the poet and he (Myers) would act as Faunus. Alta Piper, the daughter of Leonora Piper, recorded the message and mailed it to Sir Oliver in England. Not knowing what to make of it and knowing of Myers's deep interest in the classics, Sir Oliver consulted a classics scholar. He was informed that the reference was to a passage in *Horace* and that it suggested that Sir Oliver was about to experience some kind of terrible loss. In the *Horace* passage, Faunus "lightened the blow."

It was not until after he received word of Raymond's death that Lodge understood the Faunus message. His old friend Myers, in his typically schol-

Group photo with Raymond Lodge seated on ground, second from right.

arly way, was preparing him for the death of his son and letting him know that he (Myers) was there to assist Raymond.

The mediumship of Gladys Osborne Leonard began to unfold in December 1910, when she and two friends experimented with the table-tilting method of spirit communication. After numerous failures, they received messages from several people, including Leonard's mother. These messages were spelled out by the table tilting so many times for each letter of the alphabet. During this first successful sitting, a long name was spelled out, beginning with "F." As they could not pronounce it, they asked if they could abbreviate it by drawing several letters from it. The communicating entity consented and the three women selected "F-E-D-A" as the name for the entity.

Feda told them that she was Leonard's great-great grandmother, a Hindu by birth, and that she was raised by a Scottish family. She married William Hamilton, Leonard's great-great grandfather, at the age of thirteen and died soon thereafter, about 1800, while giving birth to a son. Leonard recalled hearing a story about an Indian ancestress from her mother, but did not remember any details. Feda told Leonard that she was going to con-trol her as she had work to do through her because of a great happening (apparently World War I) that would soon take place. She also told Leonard that she had been with her as a spirit guide since her birth and that she was fulfilling work required of her to make spiritual progress of her own soul. Over the next several years, Leonard progressed from table tilting to trance mediumship, as well as the direct-voice and automatic writing.

After Leonard went into trance, Feda would take over her body and begin using her speech mechanism. There was no similarity between Leonard's voice and that of Feda, who spoke like a young girl. Moreover, Feda spoke with an accent and had frequent lapses of grammar as well as difficulty in pronouncing long words. She referred to Raymond as "Yamond," to Sir Oliver as "Soliver" and Lady Lodge as "Miss Olive." Usually, Feda relayed messages from Raymond and other deceased loved ones, but occasionally she turned over control of Leonard's body to the spirit communicators so that they could speak directly without her help. She often referred to her-self in the third person, e.g., "Feda does not understand what Yaymond is telling her."

Lodge noted that in those times when Feda seemed confused by the message, her voice was reduced to a whisper and directed away from him. On several occasions, Lodge overheard Feda whisper, "What you say?" to Raymond. On another occasion, she whispered, "What, Yaymond? Al-lec." Raymond was trying to get the name, Alec, through to his father, but Feda frequently had a difficult time understanding proper names.

In Sir Oliver's first sitting with Leonard, Feda struggled to get Ray-mond's name. "Yes, I have seen him before," she told Sir Oliver, obviously referring to Lady Lodge's sitting two days earlier. "Feda remembers a letter with him too. R, that is to do with him." Then Sir Oliver heard Feda whis-per, "Try and give me another letter." Then, to Sir Oliver, she said, "It is a funny name, not Robert or Richard. He is not giving me the rest of it, but says R again; it is from him. He wants to know where his mother is; he is looking for her; he does not understand why she is not here" (Lodge 1932).

When Lady Lodge sat with Alfred Vout Peters, the same afternoon that Sir Oliver sat with Leonard, she was told by Moonstone that Raymond was referencing a photo of himself with a group of other men, one in which he was holding a walking stick. Lady Lodge could recall no such photo and when she arrived home and told Sir Oliver about the message, he also had no clue as to what photo this might be. It was not until two months later, when the mother of one of Raymond's fellow officers sent them a condolence letter and mentioned a group photo, taken twenty-one days before Raymond's death, that this message began to make sense. The woman told the Lodges that she would gladly send them a copy of the photo if they so desired one.

Lady Lodge immediately responded and requested a copy of the photograph. However, before the photograph arrived, Sir Oliver had another sitting with Leonard. He requested that Feda ask Raymond about a group photograph in which he appeared. Raymond replied that the photograph was taken outdoors and that he was sitting for it while others were standing. He further recalled someone leaning on him. Several days later, the photograph arrived in the mail. It showed three rows of officers, the back row standing, the second row sitting on a bench, and the front row sitting on the ground. Raymond was sitting on the ground, a military walking stick over his crossed legs and the arm of the officer behind him resting on his shoulder.

This was just the type of evidence Sir Oliver was looking for. It was, he concluded, Raymond's way, probably at the suggestion of Myers, of offering evidence that went beyond fraud, coincidence, or telepathy. "The elimination of ordinary telepathy from the living, except under the far-fetched hypothesis of the unconscious influence of complete strangers, was exceptionally complete, inasmuch as the whole of the information was recorded before any of us had seen the photograph," Sir Oliver offered, also mentioning that this served as a cross-correspondence of sorts in that reference to the photograph was made through one medium (Peters) while a description was given through another (Leonard) (Lodge 1932).

To further test the medium and messages, Sir Oliver asked his son Lionel, one of Raymond's five older brothers, to arrange an anonymous sitting with Leonard. On November 17, Lionel went unannounced to Leonard's home and requested a sitting. Leonard accommodated him. After she went into a trance, Feda began speaking and said that an elderly man was there to greet him. Lionel recognized the description as that of a grandfather. Feda then said a young man, about twenty-three or twenty-five was there, after which she exclaimed, "Feda knows him—Raymond. Oh, it's Raymond!" (Lodge 1932). (Lionel noted that the medium jumped about, fidgeting with her hands, just as a child would when pleased.) Feda told Lionel that Raymond was patting him on the shoulder. A conversation then ensued in which Raymond offered evidential information to convince his brother of his identity.

Raymond told Lionel that he was greeted by his Grandfather William, but that everything was vapory and vague at first. As others greeted him, they appeared to be solid and so he had a hard time grasping that he had passed over. He explained that there were houses, trees, and flowers there, and that the ground was solid. "There is something always rising from the earth plane—something chemical in form," Raymond told his brother. "As it rises to ours, it goes through various changes and solidifies on our plane" (Lodge 1932). However, he further told Lionel that he did not yet fully understand his environment but that he was making a study of it.

Raymond added that his primary occupation now was assisting new arrivals, "poor chaps literally shot into the spirit world" (Lodge 1932). Some of them, he explained, were very slow in awakening. In a later sitting, Raymond told his father that it often takes weeks for many who have passed over to realize it, as they think they are just dreaming.

Over the next few months, there were many other sittings by Sir Oliver, Lady Lodge, and other family members. Some were with mediums other than Leonard. While Sir Oliver continued to press Raymond for proof of identity, Lady Lodge was more concerned with conditions on Raymond's side of the veil. "You gravitate to a place you are fitted for," Raymond told Lady Lodge. "Mother, there's no judge and jury, you just gravitate, like to like." As for the "boys" coming over who had "nasty ideas and vices," Raymond explained that they go to a place that is something like a reformatory. "Very like your world; only no unfairness, no injustice—a common law operating for each and every one" (Lodge 1932).

By the time Sir Oliver sat with Leonard on March 3, 1916, he was convinced that she was not a charlatan, but he still felt a need to test her in various ways. Thus, he asked Raymond if he knew about "Mr. Jackson." Feda struggled with understanding Raymond's reply, but was finally able to communicate, "Fine bird, put him on a pedestal" (Lodge 1932). This was especially evidential as Sir Oliver was certain that Leonard did not know that Mr. Jackson was the name of Lady Lodge's pet peacock, nor that he had died a week earlier and was in the process of being stuffed and mounted on a wooden pedestal.

One of the more intriguing sittings took place on May 26, 1916, when Lionel and his sister, Norah, drove from the Lodge home at Mariemont, near Birmingham, to London for a sitting with Leonard. Knowing that his brother and sister were scheduled to meet with Leonard at noon, Alec Lodge, another older brother, asked two other sisters, Honor and Rosalynde (Lodge 1932), to sit with him in the drawing room and focus on asking Raymond to get the word "Honolulu" through to Lionel and Norah during their sitting with Leonard. Lionel and Norah knew nothing of this request. When Sir Oliver later read Lionel's notes of the sitting, he saw that Raymond said something about Norah playing music. Norah replied that she could not. Feda then whispered to Raymond (attention directed away from Lionel and Norah), "She can't do what?" Upon getting a response from Raymond, Feda than said, "He wanted to know whether you could play Hulu—Honolulu. Well, can't you try to? He is rolling with laughter" (Lodge 1932).

By the end of April 1916, a preponderance of evidence that Raymond had been communicating with them had been accumulated by the Lodge family. "The number of more or less convincing proofs which we have obtained is by this time very great," Sir Oliver wrote. "Some of them appeal more to one person, some to another; but taking them all together every possible ground of suspicion or doubt seems to the family to be now removed" (Lodge 1932).

Messages from Raymond Lodge

Here are some additional messages from Raymond Lodge as relayed by "Feda," the spirit control of Gladys Osborne Leonard and by "Moonstone," the spirit control of Alfred Vout Peters. All come from Sir Oliver Lodge's 1916 book, *Raymond or Life and Death* (page number in parentheses).

Adapting: "Your common-sense method of approaching the subject in the family has been the means of helping him to come back as he has been able to do; and had he not known what you had told him, then it would have been far more difficult for him to come back. He is very deliberate in what he says. He is a young man that knows what he is saying." From Moonstone to Sir Oliver Lodge on October 19, 1915 (102).

Soul travel: "He says he comes and sees you in bed. The reason for that is the air is so quiet then. You often go up there in the spirit-land while your body is asleep." From Feda to Lady Lodge on November 26, 1915 (189).

The spheres: "Such a lot of people think it's a kind of thought-world, where you think all sorts of things—that it's all you 'think.' But when you are over here you see that there's no thinking about it; it's *there,* and it does impress you with reality…The higher the sphere he went to, the lighter the bodies seemed to be—he means the fairer, lighter in colour. He's got an idea that the reason why people have drawn angels with long fair hair and very fair complexion is that they have been inspired by somebody from very high spheres."From Feda to Sir Oliver and Lady Lodge on March 24, 1916 (269).

Seeing Christ: "Mother, I thrilled from head to foot. He didn't come near me, and I didn't feel I wanted to go near him. Didn't feel I ought. The

Voice was like a bell. I can't tell you what he was dressed or robed in. All seemed a mixture of shining colours…can you imagine what I felt like when he put those beautiful rays on to me?…I don't know what I've ever done that I should have been given that wonderful experience…I can't explain it…I was overawed." Through Feda to Lady Lodge, February 4, 1916 (231).

Advancement: "He hasn't been to that place again (where he saw Christ), not that same place. But he's been to a place just below it. He's been attending lectures, at what they call, 'halls of learning'; you can prepare your-self for the higher spheres while you are living in lower ones. He's on the third (sphere), but he's told that even now he could go on to the fourth if he chose; but he says he would rather be learning the law ap-per-taining (Feda struggled with the word). to each sphere while he's living in the third, because it brings him closer—at least until you two have come over. He will stay and learn where he is." From Feda to Sir Oliver and Lady Lodge on March 24, 1916 (263).

Fifth sphere: "He went into a place on the fifth sphere—a place he takes to be made of alabaster. He's not sure that it really was, but it looked like that. It looked like a kind of temple—a large one. There were crowds passing into this place, and they looked very happy…he felt a kind of feel-ing as if he had had too much champagne—it went to his head, he felt too buoyant, as if carried a bit off the ground. That's 'cos he isn't quite attuned to the conditions…He says the old Raymond seemed far away at the time, as though he was looking back on some one else's life…Words feel power-less to describe it. He won't try." From Feda to Sir Oliver and Lady Lodge on March 24, 1916 (264).

Twelve

Claude Returns from the War

It may be objected that faith that has to be based on knowledge is no longer faith. Yes, it is, it is a stronger faith, one that can stand the onslaughts of difficulty, sorrow, and even tragedy.

—Gladys Osborne Leonard

On February 29, 1916, Mrs. L. Kelway-Bamber was on the lift of a London underground train station when she found herself standing next to Annie Brittain, a popular British medium. Brittain told Kelway-Bamber that she saw a "spirit boy" with her. She described the boy as tall, slight, and fair with blue eyes, smooth hair, well brushed off his forehead, with clear smooth skin, and boyish-looking with a very happy, merry disposition. Kelway-Bamber replied that the description exactly fit her son, Claude, who had been killed in the war three months earlier, at age 20, when the plane he had been piloting had been shot down.

On March 14, Kelway-Bamber had a sitting with Gladys Osborne Leonard, another British medium. She did not give her name or any other personal information to Leonard. After Leonard went into a trance, Feda, Leonard's spirit control, began speaking through Leonard's entranced body.

Feda told Kelway-Bamber that Claude was showing himself in a gray suit and that he was wearing it rather than his military uniform to prove to her that he was with her the previous day when she was searching for that suit. As she recorded in *Claude's Book*, which she wrote in 1919, Kelway-Bamber had been looking all over for Claude's gray suit the previous day.

Feda then told her that Claude was showing her a military medal and commented, "I don't know why he had a medal if he wasn't a soldier" (Kelway-Bamber 1919). Apparently, Feda was confused by the fact that Claude did not show himself in a military uniform. Claude then provided other evidential information through Feda to assure his mother that he was indeed there.

On April 10, Kelway-Bamber attended a public séance in which a medium, Mr. Von Bourg, was demonstrating. Kelway-Bamber had never before seen Von Bourg and the room was crowded. After speaking to several other people in the room, Von Bourg came to Kelway-Bamber and said, "There is a young airman, very happy looking, only been passed over a few months. He is tall and slight, fair smooth skin, fair hair, brushed well back, blue eyes, clear skin—do you know him?" (Kelway-Bamber 1919). Von Bourg went on to describe another boy named George and then he talked of someone named John, whom he called a "near-relative." While Kelway-Bamber immediately recognized George, she could not place John.

The following day, she again sat with Mrs. Leonard and communicated with Claude. She asked Claude if he knew who John was. "Why he's your brother, Mum!" Stunned, Kelway-Bamber replied that her brother had died at age four. "But people grow up here; they don't remain babies!" Claude replied (through Feda) (Kelway-Bamber 1919). Kelway-Bamber then pointed out that her brother would be about forty now, but the medium said he was about twenty. Claude then explained that when one grows up in the spirit world there is no material body to age.

In that and subsequent sittings, Claude went on to tell his mother about his death and his new home as well as many other things he had learned since making his transition. Concerning his death, he told her that he was on his way back from a mission over enemy lines when two enemy planes attacked him. "My observer said something, and I remember putting the nose of the machine down to get below one of our opponents, when I felt a terrible blow on my head, a sensation of dizziness and falling, and then nothing more" (Kelway-Bamber 1919). As he had no sense of time in his new body, he did not know how long before he regained consciousness in his new environment, but guessed that it might have been a fortnight or more. He recalled awakening in what appeared to be a hospital and asking what appeared to be a doctor where he was. The "doctor" explained to him that he had left his physical body. Shocked, Claude asked if that meant he was dead. "We will use that term simply as it's the only one you understand just now," the "doctor" responded. "You are alive and are starting the fuller and more beautiful life" (Kelway-Bamber 1919). A grandfather and other relatives and friends then came to greet him. Concerned about his mother, Claude was accompanied by two friends through the astral plane and found himself standing at the foot of her bed as he observed her sobbing over his death. He attempted to get her to recognize his presence but was unsuccessful. "I went to your side and put my arms round you, and though you were not conscious of my presence I seemed to be able to soothe you, for you became calmer and lay down," Claude further communicated through Feda (Kelway-Bamber 1919).

Claude went on to tell his mother that he had considered the possibility of being killed in the war and had hoped he would find himself in heaven, but it wasn't something he was looking forward to. "You know, I didn't care very much for music, and the idea of sitting on a throne clad in a white robe playing a harp sounded terribly boring," he explained (Kelway-Bamber 1919). He went on to say that he now realized that his idea of the afterlife, the one taught by orthodox religion, was erroneous, as he was experiencing a very active life in his new home, which he identified as the third sphere, or plane, sometimes referred to as "Summerland."

Among his new activities and responsibilities was greeting new arrivals from the battlefield. "We bring them away so that they may return to consciousness far from their mutilated bodies, and oh, Mum, I feel quite tired sometimes of explaining to men that they are 'dead'! They wake up feeling so much the same; some go about for days, and even months, believing they are dreaming" (Kelway-Bamber 1919).

Claude explained that death works no miracles and we wake up there the same personality that left the earth plane. The "spirit body" is a replica of the physical body, even to small details.

Besides his greeting and indoctrination responsibilities, Claude was being trained as a teacher, studying the science of life, the cause of things, and natural laws. "My duty and my business in the future is to teach as I am being taught, for every one works here as he is best fitted," Claude continued through Feda. "In helping others in some way or other, many help those they love and have left on earth, if they can get through to people there as I can to you; but for those whose relatives, either through ignorance, fear, disbelief, or religious bigotry, do not desire to get into touch with them, there is work to be done by helping less developed spirits on the lower spheres" (Kelway-Bamber 1919).

The atmosphere Claude experienced was largely of "gases," the coarser gases on the lowest spheres, the finer rising to the higher spheres with some kind of gravitation existing among them. Claude explained that his body absorbed nourishment from the gases. He got around by concentrating an effort of will within his spirit body, able to travel anywhere with the speed of thought, although he was able to simply walk around and enjoy beautiful woods and fields. He initially wondered if he was in a "thought-world," but one of his guides explained to him that it is "more real and permanent" than the one he left on the earth plane. "What makes this place so interesting is the variety of the people in it, just as the world is interesting for the same reason," Claude continued his explanation. "It would be dull if human beings were all exactly of the same stereotyped pattern physically and mentally. I think that is what made the old idea of the conventional heaven so uninviting" (Kelway-Bamber 1919).

On the first anniversary of his "death," or as he put it, his "birthday in the spirit world," Claude informed his mother that he felt as if he had been there hundreds of years, as he had learned so much. He said he had seen Christ once. "My general impression was that of brightness, almost dazzling; the air scintillated like diamonds—it almost crackled, it was so full of electricity; my feet had not a very firm grip of ground," Claude related through Feda, adding that He was not like any pictures he had ever seen of Him and that looking into His eyes created a "culminating thrill of ecstasy" (Kelway-Bamber 1919).

However, Claude went on to say that he had learned that orthodox religion offers a distorted view of Christ. "He was sent to be man's example for all time, to teach how pure and holy, and simple, and dignified, and useful, and beautiful life could be without any of the material aids of money or social position, and to prove the individual continuity of life after death," he communicated. "But He did not come to save men from the results of their sins. It is a comfortable theory, but not true" (Kelway-Bamber 1919).

Claude told his mother that he now believed in reincarnation, and that from what his guides had showed him he and his mother had been brother and sister while attached to the court of the Pharaoh thousands of years earlier. When his mother asked why conflicting information came through from the spirit world on the subject of reincarnation, he explained that souls there are still very far from understanding ultimate truth and their opinions and ideas vary just as they did on earth. "We are still learning, Mum," he said. "We have only gone a little farther along the road of experience, and have by no means reached the end of the journey. Yes, there is a heaven, but it is a long way off and has yet to be earned; even our bodies, which are still fairly material, will have to become more refined before we are fitted for that" (Kelway-Bamber 1919). He was also shown a past lifetime in which he was a woman and his mother was her best friend in Jerusalem during the early days of Christianity. In still another lifetime he was allowed to view, they were brothers living in the Balkans and leading a band of fighters.

Again talking about a typical "day" in his new life, Claude informed his mother that she often visited with him during sleep, even though she couldn't remember it when she awakened. Not everyone was able to do this, however, he told her. The person must be spiritually evolved to a certain degree. He said that his mother had been helping him in greeting new arrivals on that side during her sleep time. Claude added that he was often around at night when his father played the piano. However, rather than "hearing" the music, he "saw" it in colors.

Claude continued to stress that there was much he did not know or understand and that some of what he did understand was distorted in the process of getting it through the medium's mind. "As man evolves, he gets nearer spiritual truth, and we know here that this is infinitely greater and more wonderful than anything ever yet told," he explained. "One realizes the presentation of God usually taught on earth is utterly incorrect. He is not a glorified mortal sitting on a golden throne, not a vengeful nor jealous God—not, in a way, even a 'personal' God to be propitiated to grant special gifts to a favored few. He is not finite, but infinite; but, because it is so difficult to realize so vast a fact, we feel on earth we want to locate and limit our ideas of God to bring it within our understanding" (Kelway-Bamber 1919).

Thirteen

Dead Father and Living Son Conduct Experiments to Prove Survival

These newspaper tests are among the best pieces of carefully controlled mediumistic evidence for survival.

—Professor David Fontana

Indications are that communication between the earth plane and other realms is as much a challenge for those who have passed on to those realms as it is for us. Many of the early messages stated that scientists in those realms were just learning to manipulate matter and thus some of the methods of communication, such as rapping and table-tilting, were very crude and slow. Even after they learned how to more effectively use mediums, they encountered many obstacles in communicating with us. They persisted, however, their primary objective being to prove to us that life goes on. Some of the best evidence of this came through Gladys Osborne Leonard during sittings by the Rev. Charles Drayton Thomas, a Methodist minister.

Unlike many of his fellow clergymen, Thomas, who was called by his middle name, did not frown upon mediumship. In fact, he became an active member of the Society for Psychical Research in London during the early

1900s. He was especially interested in the theory that the medium was reading the mind of the sitter in providing information. According to Thomas, it was his father, the Rev. John Thomas, also a Methodist minister, who, posthumously, gave him the idea of what came to be known as the "book tests" and "newspaper tests." It was during a sitting with Mrs. Leonard, early in 1917, that the father and son on different sides of the veil began collaborating in the experiments.

The senior Thomas, who died in 1903, told his son that the tests had been devised by others in a more advanced sphere than his and the idea passed on to him. "The primary purpose of these efforts was said [by my father] to be a demonstration that spirit people were able to do that for which telepathy from human minds could not account, a demonstration calculated to clarify the evidence already existing for the authorship of their communication," Thomas wrote in 1922, stating that at that time he had had over a hundred sittings with Mrs. Leonard, although later in his career that number exceeded five hundred (Thomas 1948). He further mentions that the tests were secondary to other business which they discussed and that his father continually gave other evidence of his own identity.

Drayton Thomas would arrange a notebook on a table with a lighted lamp. Leonard would take a seat several feet from him and after two or three minutes of silence she would go into a trance. Suddenly, in a clear and distinct voice, Feda, Leonard's spirit control, would take over Leonard's body and begin using her speech mechanism.

Occasionally, just after Leonard went into the trance state, Thomas would hear whispering of which he could catch fragments, such as, "Yes, Mr. John, Feda will tell him…Yes, all right…" Feda often referred to herself in the third person, e.g., "Feda says she is having trouble understanding Mr. John" (Thomas 1948).

The idea behind the book tests was to communicate information gleaned by the father from a book in the son's extensive library. For example, in one of the earliest experiments, the father told the son to go to the lowest shelf and take the sixth book from the left. On page 149, three-quarters down, he would find a word conveying the meaning of falling back or stumbling. When the younger Thomas arrived home that evening after his sitting with Mrs. Leonard, he went to the book and place on the page, where he found the words, "…to whom a crucified Messiah was an insuperable stumbling-block."

The Rev. C. Drayton Thomas.

The father explained to the son, through Feda, that he was able to get the "appropriate spirit of the passage" much easier than he could the actual verbiage. He also told him that he could not make out the page numbers and so had to count the pages. However, over a period of eighteen months experimentation, he found himself able to pick up more and more words and numbers, gradually shifting from "sensing" to "clairvoyance." It was made abundantly clear by the father that he was experimenting on his side as much as his son was on the earthly side.

Realizing that his subconscious might somehow have recorded such detailed information in the book when he read it years before as well as the exact location of the book in his library, Thomas decided to experiment with books in a friend's house. He informed his father of the plan so that the father knew where to search. In one of the tests there, Feda told Thomas that on page 2 of the second book from the right on a particular shelf, he would find a reference to sea or ocean. She added that the discarnate Thomas was not sure which, because he got the idea and not the words. When Drayton Thomas pulled the book from the shelf of his friend's house, he read,

"A first-rate seaman, grown old between sky and ocean."

In another book, Drayton Thomas was told to look at page 9 where he would find a reference to changing of colors. Upon opening this book, Thomas found, "Along the northern horizon the sky suddenly changes from light blue to a dark lead colour." In still another test at his home, Feda told Drayton Thomas to go to a book at a certain point on a shelf and he would find words looking like "A-sh-ill-ee" on the cover. Feda explained that she was giving the sound but not the correct spelling. When Thomas arrived home, he went to the exact spot indicated by Feda and found a book authored by Mrs. Ashley Carus-Wilson.

Over a period of about two years, the father and son researchers carried out 348 tests. Of those, 242 were deemed good, 46 indefinite, and 60 failures. The discarnate Thomas explained the failures as his inability to get the idea through the mind of the medium or the medium's mind somehow distorting the message.

By 1919, the discarnate Thomas was moving more and more from "sensing" ideas to "seeing" through clairvoyance as he continued to experiment on his side of the veil. Later that year, through Feda, the discarnate Thomas suggested to his son that they attempt a new type of experiment, to be called the "newspaper tests." In these tests, the discarnate Thomas would provide information to be found in newspapers and magazines not yet printed. Thus, he would exercise a sort of precognition and clairvoyance. This would seemingly rule out what was being called super-ESP, the ability of the medium to go beyond reading the mind of the sitter and tap into the mind of anyone having a particular knowledge of a subject.

In a test on January 16, 1920, Thomas was told to examine the *Daily Telegraph* for the following day and to notice that near the top of the second column of the first page the name of the place he was born. Thomas was born in Victoria Terrace on Victoria Street in Tuanton. When Thomas checked the paper the following day, he found the word "Victoria" exactly where his father said it would be.

In a test on February 13, 1920, Thomas was told to go to the *London Times* of the following day and near the top of column two of the first page he would find the name of a minister with whom he (the father) had been friendly when living in Leek. Lower in the column, he would find his (Drayton's) name, his mother's name, and an aunt's name, all within a space of two inches. When the paper appeared the morning after the sitting, Thomas saw no familiar names relative to the minister friend. He then consulted with his mother who immediately called his attention to the name "Perks," informing her son that the Rev. George T. Perks was a friend of his father's and had visited him while they were living in Leek. Looking lower in the column, Thomas found his name, a slight variation of his mother's name, and an aunt's name, all within a space of 1 ¼ by 1 ½ inches.

In the same test, Thomas was told that two-thirds of the way down column one, he would find a word suggesting ammunition, and between that and the name of a former teacher of his he would find a French place name, looking like three words hyphenated into one. While Thomas found the name of a former teacher, "Watts," it was in the column next to the one indicated by his father. As for the ammunition reference, the word "canon" appeared twice, apparently taken by the discarnate Thomas as "cannon." The Belgian town of Braine-le-Château was also found in the column indicated.

Drayton Thomas checked with the *London Times* and concluded that the page from which his father took the information had not yet been type-set at the time the information was given to him through Leonard and Feda.

On April 23, 1920, Thomas was told that the deceased brother of a "medical friend" was communicating and that the surname would be found half-way down the first column of the first page of the following day's *Times*. Further, his friend's name or one almost similar to it would appear a few inches below it, and a little below would be found the name of a place which the friend and his brother had visited and very much enjoyed.

In inspecting the *Times* the following day, Thomas found his friend's name, "Dyson," exactly half-way down the column. Two inches below that

Thomas found "St. Andrew's" and later realized that "Andrews" was Dr. Dyson's middle name. Below that, he found mention of "Filey," a place where Dr. Dyson and his brother had frequently spent holidays together.

Many other newspaper tests were carried out by Drayton Thomas. In each case, he would immediately write down the information and file it in a sealed envelope with the Society for Psychical Research at a time before the type was set at the newspaper office. Further, Thomas would check papers from at least ten other days, being sure that the same names did not appear in those editions, thereby ruling out coincidence. Some of the tests were inconclusive and a few were failures, but there were many more positive results.

When Thomas asked his father how he was able to obtain information from newspapers not yet typeset, the father replied that he didn't quite understand it himself. He referred to it as some kind of "etheric foreshadowing." He likened it to seeing the shadow of a man around the corner before actually seeing the man. "Now the things I see are frequently but the spiritual counterparts of things which are about to take form; some of my tests from the *Times* might be called shadows of a substance," the discarnate Thomas explained. "When you see a shadow it is but an outline, and you do not look for detail, and that explains the difficulty of these tests; we cannot always sufficiently observe detail" (Thomas 1948). He further explained that as he had moved from sensing to seeing, he could not always see the word clearly, as in one case he gave the word "rain" for what proved to be "raisin."

Sir William Barrett, the esteemed British scientist and professor of physics in the Royal College of Science at Dublin, joined Thomas in some sittings with Leonard and experienced similar good results. In the Introduction to *Some New Evidence for Human Surival,* Barrett makes reference to the famous cross-correspondence cases, which involved disjointed messages coming through different mediums and then being pieced together, suggesting that they are too intricate to appeal to the wayfaring man. "Hence, our friends in the unseen appear to have devised the new and simpler type evidence seen in these book and newspaper tests," he wrote. "These obviously depend upon extraordinary faculties, the possession of which was not previously ascribed to the discarnate, and may indeed be exceptional among them and attained only after a time by strenuous effort" (Thomas 1948).

Barrett concluded that the cumulative effect of the evidence from the book and newspaper tests "is strongly in favour of the survival of human personality after the dissolution of body and brain."

Fourteen

Sir William Barrett Returns

I am personally convinced that the evidence we have published decidedly demonstrates (1) the existence of a spiritual world, (2) survival after death, and (3) of occasional communication from those who have passed over.

—**Sir William Barrett** (when still incarnate)

On June 6, 1925, Lady (Florence) Barrett received a letter from a member of the Society for Psychical Research (SPR) informing her that her late husband, Sir William Barrett, had communicated the previous day at a sitting with Gladys Osborne Leonard, the renowned London medium.

Sir William, an esteemed physicist, had died on May 26, 1925, at age eighty. He had served for nearly forty years as professor of physics in the Royal College of Science at Dublin and was noted for his pioneering work in iron alloys and entoptic vision. He was also the moving force behind the formation, in 1882, of the SPR, having persuaded Frederic Myers, Edmund Gurney, and Henry Sidgwick to join him in an organization to investigate paranormal phenomena. His interest in the paranormal, first made public during a talk before a scientific group in 1876, had for the most part been ignored and frowned upon by his fellow closed-minded and materialistic colleagues. Nevertheless, Barrett was able to rise above the damage to his reputation and maintain a distinguished career as a physicist and educator, being knighted in 1912.

As an obstetric surgeon and a Fellow of the Royal Society of Medicine, Lady Barrett had a scientific career and reputation of her own. In 1926, the year following her husband's death, she became Dean of the London School of Medicine for Women. Thus, even though she had shared her husband's interest in psychical research and knew of Leonard's often-tested gift, she proceeded cautiously in following up on the June 5 communication from her late husband.

The person who had informed her of her husband's messages had enclosed some notes of Sir William's comments. He asked that his wife be told that he was well and happy, that his (deceased) mother was there at the moment he passed over, and that she (Lady Barrett) would be receiving a message from him from a place "over the sea." He further mentioned that his leg was better, indicating through Leonard's motions (while in trance), from the knee upwards. The latter comment was very evidential as Lady Barrett recalled him complaining of pain in the left thigh for two days before his passing.

The "over the sea" message, Lady Barrett, later concluded, had to do with an invitation sent by Sir William on the morning he died to Mrs. Jervis, a family friend who had several sittings with Leonora Piper, the celebrated American medium, during a visit to Boston. Sir William was anxious to hear of her experiences. Mrs. Jervis received Sir William's invitation on May 27, the very day she heard of his passing. Sometime around the middle of June, Mrs. Jervis received a letter from Mrs. Piper's daughter saying that Sir William had asked Piper to inform her (Jervis) that he could not keep the appointment. Mrs. Jervis then informed Lady Barrett of this posthumous message.

Lady Barrett scheduled a sitting with Leonard on July 26, 1925. Over the next eleven years, she sat with Leonard every few months, taking verbatim notes as Sir William communicated. She also sat with several other mediums. A book, *Personality Survives Death*, published in 1937 by Longmans, Green and Co. of London, resulted from these sittings. In recording the messages, Lady Barrett did not attempt to note the dialectical nuances of Feda.

Although primarily a trance-voice medium, Leonard could also produce the direct-voice. While Feda communicated using the entranced Leonard's voice mechanism, the direct-voice involved other spirit voices from outside her body. Occasionally, Sir William's voice would break through in the direct-voice phenomenon, usually when he was trying to stress a point.

In Lady Barrett's initial sitting with Leonard, Sir William immediately came through and carried on a conversation with her, including a discussion of his final moments alive in the physical. This was very evidential, as Lady Barrett was certain Leonard could not have known the details. When Lady Barrett asked Sir William if he had met Frederic Myers, who had passed away in 1901, he replied "of course" in a very characteristic manner, stating that he had begun working with Myers in trying to improve communication from their side. He added that he had also met Sir William Crookes, another knighted British scientist and psychical researcher.

"There are two lives here: one I can tell you about and you can understand, and one I cannot tell you about till you come over," Sir William told his widow. Lady Barrett noted that these words came through in a deeper voice, very slowly, and with special emphasis, as though he were personally controlling the medium. She asked him which of the two lives was higher, and he replied that it was the one he cannot explain.

Later, after they had discussed a number of intimate affairs which Lady Barrett found too private to publish but very evidential, Feda's voice gave way to a much deeper one as Sir William slowly spoke in the direct-voice, stating, with great emphasis: "Life is far more wonderful than I can ever tell you, beyond anything I ever hoped for; it exceeds all my expectations" (Barrett 1937).

In the next sitting with Leonard, on September 20, 1925, Sir William explained what he had learned of the resurrection of Jesus, something he had been very curious about when alive. "He lived in such a way that He used spiritual forces as easily as He used material forces through His material organism, and at death there was no physical corruption of His body," Sir William explained. "So you see *His body was not there*" (Barrett 1937). Lady Barrett noted that the last five words came through in the direct-voice. He further explained that Jesus was able to raise the vibrations of the physical so that there was no body to dispose of at His death, adding that we should all be able to do it that way (if spiritually evolved enough).

Lady Barrett asked Sir William how she might satisfy people that she was really talking to him. He replied that it depends on the type of mind, commenting that reference to a tear in the wallpaper in his old room might satisfy some people and not others. Lady Barrett noted that a month before his death he had pointed out a tear in the wallpaper in one corner of his room. Sir William then said that some higher minds have gone well beyond the need for such trivial verification, mentioning another distinguished British physicist, still in the flesh, Sir Oliver Lodge. "Lodge is nearer the bigger, greater aspect of things than most," he stated (Barrett 1937).

Sir William further explained that his objective in communicating with his wife was not simply to add to the mass of evidence already given concerning the survival of consciousness at death but to help find a working philosophy to guide those on earth who are struggling with finding a purpose in life. "It seems to me from where I am most people are not even struggling but meandering on purposelessly, blindly, because they have no definite philosophy as a starting point," he said (Barrett 1937). Over the next eleven years, Sir William continued to discuss personal matters with his wife and others, occasionally bringing another discarnate soul to speak to family friends, but he increasingly talked about higher truths.

Difficulties in communication from his side of the veil were discussed during one séance. Sir William explained that when we pass over the conscious and subconscious join and make a complete mind, a mind that knows and remembers everything. However, when he slowed down his vibration to communicate with her only a portion of his mind could actually communicate. He elaborated on this by saying that the easiest things for him to remember upon entering the conditions of the sitting were ideas. Detached words, such as proper names, have no link with a train of thought. Thus, he found it much easier to express ideas on scientific interests than to remember and convey a simple name, even his own.

At a previous sitting, he had identified himself as "William" rather than "Will," which is how he was known to his wife. This made Lady Barrett wonder if it had really been her husband communicating. He explained that he simply could not get the shorter name through the medium, although with another medium he might be able to do so. Also, he had addressed his wife in a sitting as "Florrie," her childhood name, one which he had never used when alive. (He had called her "Flo.") Here again, he explained that he could not get the shorter name through the medium.

"I cannot come with and as my whole self, I cannot," Sir William said, going on to explain that he was unable to make his fourth-dimensional self exactly the same as the third and that he often lost his memory of things when communicating but then remembered them when he returned to his spirit state.

In a 1931 sitting, Sir William tried to communicate that he had recently visited with someone very close to Lady Barrett, but he could not get the name through, only the letter "B." Based on other information given, Lady Barrett concluded it was her recently deceased brother. Sir William informed her that this man had a difficult time in awakening to his new surroundings. Since he knew Sir William to be dead, he assumed he was dreaming.

Sir William mentioned that he had also met up with the famous French astronomer Camille Flammarion, another friend on earth who was deeply interested in psychical research. When Lady Barrett asked him about other planets, Sir William responded that he had not yet visited other planets but was cognizant of life on them, although a different form of life, a life that had intelligence but which differed in stature and shape to a certain extent.

Discussing the "soul body" or what he preferred to call the "etheric body," Sir William said that while we are in the flesh the subconscious locates itself in the etheric body, while the consciousness resides in the physical brain. When there is complete cooperation between the two, we have perfect sanity, perfect health, and a greater measure of happiness and wisdom because through the etheric body one reaches out to the source of inspiration and life.

Sir William said that there were lower planes than that on which he existed—depressing places populated with souls who had very little consciousness of the spiritual self while residing in the physical body. "What I want to do, and my great aim now, is to show people on earth the importance of developing the soul or etheric life before they leave the body, so that they can avoid residence in these lower planes," he communicated. "…The spiritual life must be formed in the physical life: that is the object for which God created the earth and the physical life thereon." (Barrett, 1937) He added that it is a great help if one comes over to his side attuned to an idea of what it may be like even if one isn't sure of it. Lady Barrett asked him why knowledge of the spirit world is important, suggesting that if a person simply led a good and productive life that should be enough. Sir William replied that with knowledge of it comes the ability to draw the power of the spirit through it. He likened it to a car. "You see your car; you know it's there; surely the more you *understand* your car the more you can get out of it." (The word "understand" came through in Sir William's own voice [Barrett 1937].)

Sir William went on to say that knowledge of the afterlife opens the gates of inspiration and makes the intuition keener. With that comes greater enthusiasm, greater understanding of the beauties of life, even the perception of beauty where ugliness had appeared to exist.

On the subject of prayer, Sir William said that so much of human prayer is useless because it is recited in a formal manner. A natural appeal sent out to God is much more effective than a formal prayer recited mechanically.

Moreover, if the prayer is for material advantages, it will likely not be heard.

After making his transition, Sir William rested for a little while and said he felt like a boy on a holiday exploring trip, visiting places he had only read and heard about. After he was fully adapted to his new environment, he began attending lectures in these planes, designed to assist him in evolving to higher planes. He was also involved in assisting new arrivals and studying various human diseases as well as working with Myers in studying inter-dimensional communications.

"Life on my side seems so extraordinarily easy compared to earth," Sir William offered in a 1929 sitting, "because we simply live according to the rules of love" (Barrett 1937).

Part IV
Chapters 15–22

Other Intriguing Cases of Spirit Communication

I do not hesitate to affirm my conviction, based on personal examination of the subject, that any man who declares the phenomena to be impossible is one who speaks without knowing what he is talking about; and, also that any man accustomed to scientific observation—provided that his mind is not biased by preconceived opinions—may acquire a radical and absolute certainty of the reality of the facts alluded to.

—Professor Camille Flammarion, French Astronomer

Frank R. Stockton.

Fifteen

Taking Care of Unfinished Business

Personally, I regard the fact of survival after death as scientifically proved. I agree that this opinion is not upheld in scientific quarters. But this is neither our fault nor that of the facts. Evolution was not believed until long after it was proved. The fault lay with those who were too ignorant and too stubborn to accept the facts.

—James H. Hyslop, Ph.D., LL.D.

When Frank R. Stockton died in 1902, he left a legacy of twenty-three volumes of stories for adults and children. His first book, *Ting-a-Ling*, a children's book, was published in 1870. While writing other books, including *Rudder Grange* and *The Floating Prince and Other Fairy Tales*, Stockton, who was born in Philadelphia in 1834, worked as assistant editor of *Saint Nicholas Magazine*, a magazine for children. He left that job in 1881 to become a full-time author. His most famous book, *The Lady, or the Tiger?*, was published in 1884. Because of its uncertain ending, that book would become required reading in many high school English classes, something for students to debate.

Apparently, Stockton still had a number of stories to tell when he died, because on March 23, 1909, Etta De Camp, a young New York legal secretary, received a message from Stockton by means of automatic writing. "I am Frank R. Stockton," the pencil wrote as her handwriting changed. "I have many stories I wish written out. I am glad I can write them through you. I have one I wish to write called *What Did I Do with My Wife*. We will go on with it now" (Stockton 1913).

Stockton went on to dictate (or write himself using De Camp's hand) his first short story in that first sitting. In later sittings, he would dictate another six stories, all assembled in a book published in 1913 titled *The Return of Frank R. Stockton*.

De Camp knew nothing about automatic writing until January or February 1909 when she read a newspaper article by William T. Stead of London about his experience as an automatic writer. She was intrigued and decided to give it a try, patiently sitting with pad and pencil. After some time, she felt a "thrill" go from her shoulder to her fingertips as though she had been touched by an electric battery. "To my utter amazement the pencil began to move," she recalled. "I watched it, fascinated, for I was absolutely sure I was not moving it myself. It seemed as though my arm and hand had become detached from my body and did not belong to me" (Stockton 1913).

At first, she got only circles and scrolls, then some illegible words. It was not until her third night of experimenting that the writing became readable and expressed thought. The first message came from an Indian calling himself "Blackfoot." That was followed by a message from "Lafayette." Whether it was the famous man by that name, De Camp did not know. Another Indian who gave his name as "Three Feathers" then signed in. A week or two later, she received several messages from her father, who had died twelve years earlier. The messages were for her mother and contained many details that De Camp knew nothing about. However, her mother confirmed them as fact.

De Camp was informed that they were writing through the "law of vibration." She wrote in the dark as light disturbed her. The slightest noise sounded like the firing of a cannon. She recalled fighting off the trance condition, but recorded that she was in an abnormal state when the writing

Etta De Camp.

came through. She had no idea what the next word would be until she saw it on the paper. In one case, as "she" wrote the words "Who said we were d…," she assumed the last word would be "dead," but was surprised when the word turned out to be "drunk," which proved to her that her conscious mind had nothing to do with the writing.

After Stockton first took control of her pencil on March 23, De Camp felt intense pain in the forehead between her eyes, "and I felt a sensation in the left side of my head as though another mind was crowding into my own." However, the pain subsided and the first story was completed. Three days later, Stockton wrote another story, *My Wireless Horse*. He advised De Camp that best results could be obtained if she would write an hour or two each morning at a fixed time. He told her that when she felt a pain behind her ears it would be a sign that he was ready to write. He explained that he was anxious to go on to the next plane, but that his brain had to be relieved of the stories before he could progress further. "We must be freed from all earth vibrations before we can go on," he wrote through De Camp's hand. "The mind carries too many memories for me to get free. I must write out my book and my stories before I can get beyond the earth-vibrations which keep me here" (Stockton 1913).

Prior to becoming an instrument for Stockton, De Camp knew nothing about him, although she had read *The Lady, or the Tiger?* during her school years. She claimed only a faint recollection of it. While apparently realizing that subconscious memories could not be completely ruled out, De Camp was certain she had no creative literary ability of her own and that she was not controlling the pencil. Moreover, she claimed that she never saw the stories in her imagination and had never really cared for humorous stories, even as a child. She further recalled that she often resisted the writing sessions, and when she did she would awaken in the morning in a dazed condition, as though drugged. She felt as though she were enveloped in a thick fog. The greater she resisted, the stronger the force became until she was finally compelled to take the pencil and write in order to find relief.

Upon learning of her experiences, some friends cautioned her about continuing. She was told that there were low-level spirits who delight in masquerading under the name of some well-known person and that the spirit claiming to be Frank R. Stockton might very well be one of them. If that was possible, she reasoned, then it must be equally possible for an honest spirit to represent itself. "I have never for one moment doubted the genuineness of the spirit claiming to be that of Mr. Stockton," De Camp reported. "The serious objects of his return, the development of some higher sense enabling me to feel the personality of this entity so strongly, and to know its characteristics so well, make Mr. Stockton, to me, as real as anyone I know in earth-life" (Stockton 1913).

At a sitting on August 5, 1909, Stockton wrote that he had been searching for years for the right person to continue his stories. "I am very fortunate in finding you, my dear madam, as you are sensitive to my vibration, and so I reach you easily," he informed her. "We are in perfect accord, and, together, will do a great work, and teach the old world what can be done even after the so-called end of man" (Stockton 1913).

At times, De Camp had difficulty in achieving the passive state necessary for effective communication. Stockton told her not to think at all while writing, as best results were obtained when the conscious mind was not allowed to interfere with the subconscious. "The struggle for me to overcome the opposition of your conscious mind has been very great," Stockton counseled her. "The strain on you has been severe also" (Stockton 1913).

Apparently, Stockton still held on to his ego as he insisted that De Camp not take credit for the stories or pass herself off as the author. "These stories are not yours nor do they belong to anyone living on your plane," he admonished her. "They are mine and I shall never consent to their being sold under any other name" (Stockton 1913). He also asked that ten percent of the proceeds from the sale of any book be given to his estate.

When De Camp questioned the frivolous and humorous nature of the stories, Stockton explained that his objective was to show that people passing from the body to other planes of existence do not suddenly change temperament and personality. "I am no more capable of writing serious stuff now than when in the body, and if these stories were not written in a humorous style they would not be recognized as mine."

Stockton further told De Camp that he felt like a clown at the circus because some of the greatest writers the world has ever known were waiting to find an instrument through which they could write.

Dr. James H. Hyslop, a retired Columbia University professor of logic and ethics who took over as head of the American Society for Psychical Research and reorganized it after the death of Dr. Richard Hodgson in 1905, heard the story about De Camp and Stockton and decided to investigate. He was informed by Henry Alden, the editor of *Harper's Monthly*, that the stories produced by De Camp's hand were sufficiently like those of Stockton for him to say that they were "very real." John R. Meader, who had studied Stockton, claimed that they were "very characteristic" of Stockton's writing when he was alive. At the time, Hyslop was studying the mediumship of Minnie Meserve Soule, who was given the pseudonym "Mrs. Chenoweth" to protect her privacy. Therefore, Hyslop arranged for De Camp to travel to Boston and have an anonymous sitting with Soule. He did not bring her into the room until Soule was in a trance state and had her leave before Soule recovered normal consciousness.

An entity giving his name as Frank Richard Stockton and saying that his real Christian name was "Francis" communicated through Soule. Neither De Camp nor Hyslop knew that Richard was his middle name or that Francis was his given name. He told them that he had died in Washington, D.C. during the month of April and then discussed at some length the work he was doing through De Camp, confirming that he was the source of her stories, adding that her subconscious sometimes distorted the stories, though not to any great extent.

Hyslop observed that there were many touches of personal character and wit coming through, and when he told Stockton that he wanted more evidence of personal identity in order to silence the skeptical critics, Stockton replied: "I really have a desire to do a certain kind of work, but deliver me from the class who cut up their relatives to see how their corpuscles match up…I think I won't do for your business at all, but personally I have no fight with you. You can go on and save all the critics you can, but don't send them to me when they die…For I would make no heavenly kingdom for them. I had my share of them while I lived, and I wash my hands of the whole lot" (Stockton 1913).

Stockton then asked Hyslop if he knew the Irishman's toast. When Hyslop replied that he wasn't familiar with it, Stockton gave the toast: "May you live to see the green grass growing over your grave." After Stockton departed, George F. Duysters, who had been an international lawyer and De Camp's employer before his death, began speaking through Mrs. Soule. Duysters had previously communicated with De Camp through her hand and during one of those communications had discussed a trip to the mountains that De Camp had made with Duysters and his family. Prior to his death, he started to draw a scene where they had camped, but because of his death it was never finished. While communicating through De Camp's hand, Duysters asked her to fetch the picture so that he could finish it. She did so and Duysters did finish the drawing. Hyslop was aware of this before the sitting with Soule and asked Duysters if he recalled the picture. Duysters replied that he did and then described the picture.

"It is especially significant that both personalities should appear to communicate," Hyslop reported. "They are not in any way connected with each other in life, and neither of them were relatives of Miss De Camp" (Stockton 1913).

In concluding the 1913 book, De Camp wrote that she would never have volunteered for such a project as it caused too much pain and suffering. In his final communication to De Camp, Stockton commented: "Even if we can convince but a few of the continuity of life, we will have done a great work." (Stockton, 1913)

Sixteen

The Education of a Skeptic

It seems to me the facts are undeniable. I am convinced that I have been present at realities. Certainly I cannot say in what material- ization consists. I am ready to maintain that there is something pro- foundly mysterious in it which will change from top to bottom our ideas on nature and life.

—**Dr. Charles Richet** (1913 Nobel Prize Winner in medicine)

After reading *The Shadow World*, a 1908 book in which author Hamlin Gar- land reported on his investigation of mediums, Harvard professor William James told Garland that he envied him because he had found so many good mediums. James, while having studied Leonora Piper, the renowned Boston medium, said he had not been so successful in locating others.

When, in 1891, Garland was asked to join the ranks of the American Psychical Society (APS) of Boston as an investigator, he protested, com- menting that he believed in positive sciences. As a student of Darwin and Herbert Spencer, Garland took pride in his agnosticism and skepticism. He was surprised and amused that he would be asked to participate in investi- gations of what he referred to as the "dark side of the moon." But after it was pointed out to him that the organization wanted young, open-minded skeptics as their investigators to offset what might be seen as credulity among some of the older investigators, Garland consented.

During his lifetime (1860-1940), Garland authored fifty-two books, including a biography of Ulysses S. Grant. He won the 1922 Pulitzer Prize for *A Daughter of the Middle Border*. A friend of President Theodore Roosevelt, poet Walt Whitman, and author Henry James, he was intimately involved with major literary, social, and artistic movements in American culture. In 1926, the University of Wisconsin awarded him an honorary Doctor of Letters degree. He was later awarded honorary doctorates by Beloit College, Northwestern University and the University of Southern California, the latter's Doheny Memorial Library now housing the Hamlin Garland Collection. The Hamlin Garland Society exists today to disseminate information on Garland's literary works, and his early home in West Salem, Wisconsin, is a national historic landmark and museum. He had a keen mind and was not someone to be easily duped.

In *Forty Years of Psychic Research*, published in 1936, Garland tells of his many investigations of mediums. While he felt certain that he had ruled out fraud in many cases, he was reluctant to subscribe to the spirit theory and, concomitantly, to life after death. He still clung to his earlier theory that mediumistic phenomena were somehow unwittingly produced by the subconscious of the mediums. When communication was supposedly coming from a discarnate soul, he wondered if the medium had telepathic powers and was unconsciously tapping into the memories of the person sitting with the medium. When there were physical manifestations, he wondered if the medium had produced them through some kind of subconscious telekinetic powers. He ended *Forty Years* by saying he could come to no conclusions as to the cause or origin of the phenomena as he simply could not comprehend a "fourth dimension." He ended the book with a somewhat guarded statement: "I concede the possibility of their [spirits'] persistence, especially when their voices carry, movingly, characteristic tones and their messages are startlingly intimate. At such times, they seem souls of the dead veritably reimbodied. They jest with me about their occupations. They laugh at my doubts, quite in character. They touch me with their hands" (Garland 1936).

On November 10, 1893, a séance was held at the Boston home of Professor Amos Dolbear, a fellow APS investigator. Dolbear was head of the department of astronomy and physics at Tufts College and had been credited with inventing the static telephone and an electric gyroscope used to demonstrate the earth's rotation. Only Garland, Dolbear, Dolbear's wife, and the

Hamlin Garland.

medium, Mary Curryer Smith, were present. (Out of privacy concerns, Garland assigned her the pseudonym "Mrs. Smiley" in his books.) Smith was a direct-voice medium. Such mediums use a megaphone or "trumpet" to amplify the voices of the spirits. Often the trumpet, held by invisible hands, floats around the room and stops in front of the sitter for whom the message is intended. Voices much different than the medium's are usually heard, occasionally in languages unknown to the medium. When Garland first learned of this phenomenon, he suspected that it was all a hoax carried out by means of ventriloquism. However, many years of testing and examining such mediums convinced him that at least many of them were for real.

Garland had discovered Smith while lecturing in Santa Barbara, California. He was so impressed by her that he arranged for the APS to pay her expenses to Boston so that she could be tested. As darkness was required, Garland, in order to rule out fraud, tied Smith to her chair, binding both her arms and her ankles with strong tape. He also draped newspaper over her knees and tacked the edges to the floor so that any movement could be detected by the crackle. While Garland kept a hand on one of the medium's wrists, Dolbear kept his hand on the other. An hour or so passed without result, and Dolbear was prepared to call it a night, feeling that the safeguards against fraud had stifled the medium. However, Garland was accustomed to waiting as long as four hours for phenomena to manifest and convinced Dolbear to wait a little longer. Soon thereafter, books from Dolbear's library began whizzing over their heads and landing on the table in front of them. Some two dozen books were stacked by shadowy hands. There was enough light for Garland to see the hands. He recorded that they were clearly those of a man and much larger than the medium's. A spirit named "Wilbur" began speaking through the medium's megaphone or "cone," which floated around the room.

Garland recorded that the cone rose high in the air when Wilbur identified himself as Jefferson Wilbur Thompson, a brigadier general in the Confederate army who died in Jefferson City after the Civil War. He said he was one of the medium's "guides." According to Garland, he spoke in a manly voice and as clearly as if he were a living human being. Wilbur carried on for two hours, keeping the sitters laughing with frequent "wise-cracking." During all of the activity, Garland monitored Smith's position and noted that she remained in a "deathly trance."

After the books had been stacked on the table, Mrs. Dolbear asked Wilbur if he could bring the small candy box on the shelf above the books. Professor Dolbear called her request "preposterous," but a moment later the box was laid upon the table. Garland asked Wilbur to write his name in one of the books on the table. When the phenomena stopped and the lights were turned on, one of the books was found to have Wilbur's signature.

Before the lights were turned on, however, Mrs. Dolbear appeared to fall into a trance and become clairvoyant. She said that she could see forms moving about the room and then the voice of a deceased relative began speaking to her. According to Garland, the conversation went on for some time.

As Garland apparently assumed that "Wilbur" was a secondary personality of the medium and was using subconscious telekinetic powers to move the books and the cone, he did not concern himself with attempting to confirm the existence of Jefferson Wilbur Thompson. A recent Google search revealed that there was a Brigadier General Meriwether Jefferson Thompson in the Confederate army and that he died in 1876. Another site mentions that "General Jefferson Thompson" surrendered to General Granville Dodge in Arkansas. The name "Wilbur" is not mentioned in either case, but this could very well have been a nickname, especially for someone who did not care for the name Meriwether.

During the autumn of 1907, Garland was a guest at the home of John O'Hara Cosgrave, the editor of *Everybody's Magazine*, a popular publication of the time. Cosgrave informed Garland that his friend, a Dr. Turner, had told him of some amazing psychic feats by a young lawyer named Daniel Peters and wanted someone else to witness and test them. Several days later, Garland, Cosgrave, and Peters were guests at Turner's home. Peters told Garland that he was working for a big Wall Street company and did not want his name in print because he feared the company might fire him if they knew he was a medium. He further said he had been aware of his powers since about the age of four and that his deceased grandfather and a deceased friend named "Evans" were the ones who most often came to him. Peters added that when he thought toward a person, he found himself "all around him—inside of him at times."

After the small group formed a circle and dimmed the lights, Evans announced himself by tapping on the table. Sitters on both sides of Peters held his hands to confirm that he was not making the noise. A few moments later, the table inside the circle began rising, went over their heads and dropped softly outside the circle. The sitters returned the table to its former position and again dimmed the lights. There was paper in the center of the table and they heard the sound of writing. Garland heard the tearing of paper and it was thrown over to him by invisible hands. Upon turning up the lights, Garland observed the signature of his deceased father-in-law, Professor Taft, in the peculiar handwriting that was his when alive. Garland recorded that he had not been thinking of his father-in-law, had not attempted to visualize his signature, and was certain that no one in the circle knew that Taft was related to him. Turner found the signature of his brother, exactly in his brother's handwriting.

In a second sitting with Peters, Garland took every possible precaution to rule out fraud. He tied Peters to a chair with a spool of dental floss, being sure his wrists were securely bound. As an extra precaution, Garland tied the sitter on Peters's right to Peters, while he (Garland) sat on his left. After the lights were turned out, Garland noticed a faint, bluish, smoke-like cloud developing in front of Peters. A hand darted out of the cloud and firmly grabbed Garland's left wrist. This spectral hand then darted to the center of the table and took hold of a glass, lifting it to Peters's mouth so that he could drink. All the while, Garland controlled Peters's left hand and the sitter on his right controlled his right hand. Garland was certain that Peters had no accomplice. There was enough light for Garland to see the phantasmal arm clothed in gray vapor.

At a third sitting with Peters, Garland nailed Peters's clothing to the chair and again bound him with dental floss. A phantom appeared and spoke to the man next to Garland in Polish. The man stated that it was his brother. When that spirit faded out, Evans, Peters's guide, materialized and offered Garland his hand. Garland observed that the hand was "cobwebby" in texture and appeared to melt away. He felt its bones for a moment and when he released his grip the figure vanished like a bubble. Soon, another figure appeared, standing at attention like a soldier. Garland could clearly see this phantom form and noticed that he had no perceptible feet. "He gave the impression of a form suspended—unfinished—in the air and yet with bulk," Garland wrote (Garland 1936). The phantom bowed to Garland three times before moving toward Peters and then seemingly vanished into Peter's body. Peter then fell "like a log" on the floor.

On a visit to Chicago in 1907, Garland was introduced to a Mrs. Herbein (to whom Garland gave the pseudonym "Mrs. Hartley"), another amateur medium who did not want public exposure but who agreed to be tested. She explained to Garland that her mediumship was frowned upon by her neighbors and that her son's friends taunted him because of her gift, although she questioned whether it was a gift, as the spirits were always with her and often prevented her from sleeping. She added that evil spirits sometimes harassed her.

Mrs. Herbein was primarily an independent writing medium who worked in the light and did not go into trance. Writing would take place with powdered pencils inserted between the leaves of book slates, the phenomenon believed to be carried out by spirits, although Garland still clung to a mechanistic theory involving the subconscious and telepathy along with telekinetic powers. In his very first sitting with Herbein, Garland received a message from his old friend, Edward MacDowell, a composer, who had died several months earlier. "I would that you could see me as I am now, still occupied and happy to be busy," MacDowell wrote (Garland 1936). While Mrs. Herbein attended to something in the kitchen, Garland put a question to MacDowell on some paper, folded it several times and kept it hidden from the medium. He asked if MacDowell could give him a bar from his *Sonata Tragica* as a test. When the medium returned, Garland heard the sound of writing on the slates and when he opened the slates, he found that his request had been granted with two bars of music. He continued to receive more music on other slates and then heard a whisper which seemed to come from the air a foot or two above the medium's head. "These notes are from the third movement of my *Sonata Tragica*," the voice declared (Garland 1936). While considering ventriloquism by the medium and telepathy as to the question he had put to MacDowell, along with the possibility that Herbein could actually write music and knew more about music than she had disclosed, Garland was certain she could not have recorded the music on the slates as they were in his possession the entire time.

MacDowell had signed several slates with "E. A. McDowell" and with an unusual flourish. Garland wondered why he would have misspelled his own name, but when he later spoke with MacDowell's widow he was informed that McDowell was his given name and that the "a" was added for some unexplained professional reason early in his career. Mrs. MacDowell also told Garland that her husband had used the "boyish" flourish when she first met him and that the signature appeared to be his.

Some years later, while living in New York City, Garland was having lunch with his old friend Edwin Winter, a retired railroad executive, at the Bankers' Club on Wall Street when Winter told him about Tom Traynor, a man with "second sight." Winter related that on one occasion Traynor told him that a man giving his name as "Milton K. Smalley" was there. Traynor described Smalley as a "queer, seedy, old chap, who said he was 'kind of an uncle'" to Winter. He told Winter that he was married to his Aunt Sarah when he (Winter) was a child. Winter recalled such a marriage, but had forgotten about the man. Winter then asked Traynor what Smalley wanted. Smalley informed him that he didn't want anything, that he simply wanted to set the record straight. Smalley explained that he didn't appreciate Winter's aunt and enlisted in one of the first Massachusetts regiments to go South during the Civil War. He was then killed in Baltimore along with four other men.

Upon attempting to verify this information with the Adjutant General in Boston, Winter was told that no such man could be found on the rolls of the regiment that marched through Baltimore. At another meeting with Traynor, Winter informed him of his investigation. Traynor then went into what appeared to be a trance state, and Smalley began to talk. He told Winter that because he was leaving his aunt and going with another woman, he enlisted as Jackson Turner. Winter then went back to the Adjutant General and confirmed that a man named Jackson Turner had enlisted in that regiment and had been killed in the streets of Baltimore with three other men.

Interested in meeting Traynor, Garland asked Winter if he could arrange a sitting with him. The meeting took place at Winter's Park Avenue apartment with Mrs. Garland accompanying her husband. As they were sitting at the fireplace over coffee and cigars following dinner, Traynor told Mrs. Garland that a young woman was standing beside her. He said that she gave her name as "Carrie L. Scales" and was tall with brown hair combed up in a roll above her brow, appearing to be about thirty-five. Mrs. Garland immediately recognized the woman as an old friend. Traynor then began to impersonate the deceased woman. It was as if she were using his organs of speech. She spoke to Mrs. Garland of many personal details, some of which Mrs. Garland was not aware of until she later checked them out. Traynor then turned abruptly to Winter and told him that a man was there who had known him since he was a boy. The man said he was a conductor on the local which ran from Chicago to Madison and that he recalled Winter as the little boy who came down to the platform of the station at Beloit, Wisconsin, to sell berries to the passengers. "After you became a big man in the railway business you made me a division superintendent," he told Winter. "That was a mistake. I wasn't big enough for the job" (Garland 1936).

Winter turned to Garland and told him that he remembered the man perfectly, but that he hadn't thought of him in years. He said he did sell berries on the Beloit platform and remembered the conductor for his fancy vest and the way he would swing onto the last train car. After becoming general manager of the Northern Railway, he promoted him, but the man failed as a supervisor and returned to being a conductor.

While Garland considered the possibility that Traynor was telepathically digging into subconscious minds, he wondered how information unknown to his wife and Winter could have been obtained by Traynor.

Years later, on January 22, 1933, Garland and his wife were living in Los Angeles and sitting with Delia Drake, a long-time acquaintance who had developed into a direct-voice medium. After the lights were turned off and some songs sung, Drake's trumpet, which had luminous paint on it, rose in the air and came to Garland, waving up and down. The name "Fuller" came through in a faint whisper. Garland recognized it as his old friend, Henry B. Fuller. The trumpet then floated to Garland's daughter and a whispered voice identifying itself as "Charles Francis" spoke. It was Charles Francis Browne, his daughter's brother-in-law.

The trumpet then moved in front of Olive Grismer, who heard her deceased sister speak while sobbing. While Garland knew Drake to be a sincere and religious woman, he knew that skeptics would say that since she had known Garland and his wife for more than thirty years that she could have found out about Fuller and Charles Francis. However, he was certain that Drake knew nothing of Grismer and her sister and saw the only possibility as mindreading or actual spirit communication. But, if mindreading, how did the medium's mind dramatize it by turning it into a dialogue?

At a later sitting in Garland's study, Fuller again communicated. Garland said they conversed just as they had when he was in the flesh, that the utterances from the trumpet were concise, humorous, and keenly intellectual, entirely in character with the person he had known. At another sitting, a week later, two invisibles whispered their names to Mrs. Garland. One was a relative by marriage and the other her daughter. The daughter spoke in a wistful and eager way, just as they had remembered her. Fuller returned, but Garland struggled to understand him. Fuller explained that articulation was difficult.

At still another sitting, Fuller brought William James, who had died in 1910, to communicate. Garland wrote that James spoke to him with a great deal of feeling in a husky whisper but with poor articulation so that he could not distinguish some of the words. Theodore Roosevelt also came through and conversed with Garland, as did another former president, Franklin Pierce, a distant relative of Mrs. Garland.

A month or more went by before their next sitting with Drake. Fuller again communicated. He explained that those on his side of the veil had a sense of continuity of events but not of time divided into periods. Garland asked him what the fourth dimension meant to him. Fuller replied that it was a plane just beyond the three-dimensional plane known to Garland. Garland told him that he could not grasp the concept of a fourth dimension, to which Fuller asked, "What would a two-dimensional man make of a cube?" (Garland 1936). Fuller also chastised Garland for his refusal to accept the spirit hypothesis.

Theodore Roosevelt, Walt Whitman, Sir Arthur Conan Doyle, and William James, all friends of Garland, communicated at later sittings. When James attempted to explain the conditions which surrounded him, he said, "Can a fish explain how he breathes and swims?" Still, Garland doubted. "I have no conclusion," he wrote, still clinging to the subconscious, telepathy, and telekinetic theories. "I am still the seeker, still the questioner" (Garland 1936). It was not until he encountered the mystery of the buried crosses, discussed in the next chapter, that Garland began to lean heavily toward the spirit hypothesis.

Seventeen

The Mystery of the Buried Crosses

*Hundreds, yea thousands [of spirits], have come and talked with
me, and to many whom I have invited to participate in the work—
thousands of different voices with different tones, different thoughts,
different personalities, no two alike; and at times in different languages.*

—**Edward C. Randall, Esq.**

In his 1939 book, *The Mystery of the Buried Crosses*, Hamlin Garland (Garland 1939), a Pulitzer prize-winning author, explained that shortly after giving a talk on psychic phenomena in Los Angeles in 1934 he received a letter from one Gregory Parent about the strange psychic happenings in the
life of his wife, Violet, who had died five years earlier. He related that "dead
souls" began conversing with her in 1914, and that they had led her to a
number of buried "treasures," mostly Indian artifacts.

Parent, who had lived with his wife in Redlands, California, some sixty
miles east of Los Angeles, said that his wife had been "strangely gifted" from
birth, but it wasn't until after an illness in 1914 that she began going into
trance and seeing and communicating with spirits, one of whom was Father

Junipero Serra, the famous California missionary. He also informed Garland that his wife had taken a number of spirit photographs.

Curious, Garland visited Parent in his Redlands home and saw the strange photographs of spirits standing around the humble furnishings of the Parent home. He observed that they were all made with a cheap camera and printed on poor paper. One of the figures was William T. Stead, the famous British journalist and medium who went down with the *Titanic*. Garland had known Stead and could not believe that he would have posed in such an "absurd costume." Other pictures were of mission priests and Indians. Garland closely examined the photographs and did not know what to make of them. He also noted that Parent had several bundles of notebooks documenting the story and the many trips he and his wife had taken to find the buried treasures.

Parent wondered if Garland might be interested in writing a book about this strange story. Garland told him that he wanted to hear more of the story, but he needed to finish a book he was working on at the time. When, in 1936, he attempted to recontact Parent, he discovered that Parent had died. After several months of inquiry, Garland found that Parent's collection of photos and manuscripts had passed into the possession of a half-sister, Louise Stack, of Moorpark, California. He contacted her and she turned over boxes of papers and photographs to him while leading him to a small carpenter's shop where there were stored seventeen glass-topped cases filled with crosses and other relics, all neatly arranged. Mrs. Stack turned over custody of the papers, photographs, and some 1,500 relics to Garland.

As Garland would gather from studying the papers, the Parents began finding gold and silver coins as well as currency and other treasures in tin cans, rotted pocketbooks, and various containers buried in places all around southern and central California. They found enough money to buy a house and provide a standard of living beyond what Gregory's job as a grocery clerk would have permitted. For ten years, from 1914 until 1924, Father

A few of the buried crosses in the West Salem Museum.

Serra, other deceased missionary priests, and long-dead Indians gave Mrs. Parent instructions on how to locate the buried caches, the purpose being to provide evidence of life after death. What other than spirit communication might explain the Parents being able to find such artifacts in dozens of places over thousands of square miles?

In studying the twenty-two notebooks left by Parent, Garland concluded that "this little grocer's clerk, in his bungling and tedious way, had honestly tried to make a scientific statement of his experiences as the husband of a woman who walked with spirits" (Garland 1939). He described Parent as an obscure, illiterate, and poor man who felt it was his sacred duty to make the story known and spread a belief in the return of the dead. Garland found no evidence that Parent was trying to profit from the story.

Parent had noted that the "dead souls" led them to the money and other valuables only to help them carry on the work of finding the crosses and miscellaneous other relics, which had no real monetary value. These trinkets had been buried by the Indians when the missions were threatened by the Mexicans. They were usually encased in balls of adobe so that they could not be distinguished from common rocks.

Parent also recorded that the spirits came to his wife night after night to give directions on how to reach the burial places. As the Parents had no car, they were accompanied by friends and neighbors. Once having reached the area designated by the spirits, Violet would walk around until a "strange chill" came over her. She would then say something like, "We will find thirty crosses here." They would dig and find the predictions were accurate. It took them nine years and three thousand miles of motoring all over southern and central California to find the relics.

His curiosity further aroused, Garland set out to find the friends and neighbors in Redlands who assisted the Parents in their discoveries. While many of them had died or moved away, he did locate fifteen people and found them all to be credible witnesses. One man, who operated a business, recalled being very skeptical when Mrs. Parent told him that there were crosses under a large boulder. Using crowbars, two men moved the boulder, under which they found three crosses.

Over the next six months, Garland corresponded with five museums, including the Smithsonian and one in Mexico City, but they were all skeptical and, strangely, not interested in the relics. Apparently, they did not believe that the Indians had metallic objects and therefore concluded that they were fakes. Even though they had no apparent monetary value, Garland felt that confirmation of the story would go a long way toward proving life after death, as apparently that is what the spirits and the Parents set out to do in the first place. Having had many years of experience with mediums, he decided to find one who might put him in touch with Violet Parent and request her help in finding additional relics, as Gregory Parent had noted that there were, according to the spirits, more to be found. Sometime around July 1937, Garland selected Sophia Williams, an amateur medium who did not charge for her services, to help him in his search.

Williams was a "direct-voice" medium, but unlike most of the direct-voice mediums, she did not require darkness and did not go into a trance. She would place the larger end of the megaphone against her breast while Garland would listen for voices at the smaller end and relay them to a stenographer. In his very first "sitting" with Williams, Garland was greeted by one of his oldest friends, Henry B. Fuller, who had helped him research cases of mediumship when

Medium Sophia Williams.

he was alive. Always on the lookout for fraud, Garland wondered if Williams had read of Fuller in his book, *Forty Years*. A few minutes later, another voice was heard. The spirit identified himself as Lorado, his wife's brother, who had died the previous year.

Garland noted that Fuller called him by his last name, while Lorado addressed him by his first name, exactly as they had done when they were alive. He further noted that the voices, which were high in vibration, sometimes seemed to be coming from the megaphone and at other times from the air above the medium's head.

The most convincing evidence came when a voice addressed the stenographer, Gaylord Beaman. "Gay, this is Harry," the voice was heard. When asked for a last name, "Friedlander" was given. The astonished Beaman explained to Garland that Harry Friedlander was a friend who died in a plane crash in San Francisco Bay. The spirit then gave some details concerning the crash. Garland was certain that Williams knew nothing of Beaman and could not have researched this information beforehand. Garland then asked Fuller if he could contact Violet Parent. Fuller replied that he would try, but it would have to be at another sitting.

Two days later, the second sitting took place. Garland first heard a voice say, "This is Turck, Dr. Turck." Turck went on to tell Garland that he (Turck) was an "old fool" for having called Garland's psychical research so much "humbuggery" when he was alive. Here again, Garland concluded that the medium could have known nothing about Turck's attitude, which had been expressed at a luncheon.

After the first few sittings with Williams, Garland devised a transmitting box with sixty feet of wire connected to another box containing a receiver and amplifier. The purpose was to isolate Williams from his questions to the spirit communicators and thereby completely rule out mental telepathy. With Williams two rooms away and behind closed doors in Garland's home, Williams could neither hear Garland's questions nor see what he was pointing to or looking at, and since the spirits answered him with detailed information, Garland concluded that this was further evidence that Williams was not drawing the information from his or the stenographer's mind.

When Garland's "Uncle David," who had been dead for some thirty years, communicated, Garland asked him if he remembered the old tune he used to play for him in on his fiddle. Through the amplifier, Garland then heard the tune "When you and I were young, Maggie" being whistled and played on a fiddle. It was not the tune Garland had in mind, so Garland ruled out the possibility that his subconscious mind was communicating with Williams's subconscious. Moreover, if Williams were a fraud, she would have had to know about Uncle David, anticipate Garland's question to him about the tune, and smuggle a fiddle into and out of Garland's home.

When the voice changed, Garland asked the speaker to identify himself. "Doyle," the voice replied. It was Sir Arthur Conan Doyle, the creator of Sherlock Holmes, another psychical researcher known to Garland when he was alive. Doyle said that Sir William Crookes and Dr. Gustave Geley,

Hamlin Garland digging for crosses while Sophia Williams looks on.
Photo courtesy University of Southern California Library, Hamlin Garland Collection

two more famous psychical researchers who had died, were there with him. They all spoke and said they were there to help Garland communicate with their side of the veil. Geley began speaking in French until Garland told him that he was not fluent in French. Geley then switched to English. Professor William James also spoke, but Garland was unable to understand what James was saying.

More spirits came, including one who identified himself as Harry Carr, another of Beaman's friends. Carr asked Beaman to contact his friend Lee Shippey to see if his manuscript might now be published. Here again, this was highly evidential as the names and information were well beyond the scope of research.

Garland's old friend Burton Babcock then communicated. Garland described Babcock's speech as "hesitating and incoherent," which was characteristic of him when he was alive. Rudyard Kipling broke in at one point, speaking Gaelic before switching to English with an Irish brogue. William Stead also came through and confirmed that the photo in Mrs. Parent's album was genuine, commenting that he used to wear the cloak that Garland thought looked "absurd."

Indeed, it appeared that a whole group of people, including some very famous ones had gathered on the other side to avail themselves of Williams's mediumship. It was not until the third sitting that Violet Parent spoke. She told Garland that there were more crosses to be discovered and that because she was "ig-ne-runt" she would ask Father Serra to direct Garland in his search.

Other spirits totally unrelated to Garland's search continued to speak at times. One identified herself as Leila McKee, an old Wisconsin acquaintance. Another Wisconsin acquaintance, Wendell McIldowney, also came through. While Garland had by this time concluded that Williams was not a charlatan, he knew he had to be ready for claims by skeptics that Williams had done some research before meeting him. It would have been virtually impossible, he concluded, for any researcher to turn up either of these names from his past.

Still, Garland wondered if Williams was somehow unknowingly tapping into his subconscious. However, he reasoned that his subconscious could not possibly be involved in directing Williams to uncover additional crosses or other artifacts. If the spirits could help him uncover more artifacts, that would, Garland concluded, be solid proof of the existence of a spirit world and, concomitantly, life after death.

Before Father Serra began communicating, Conan Doyle brought George Parker Winship, an ethnologist when he was alive, to comment on the crosses. Winship explained that some of them were from Central America—from Yucatan and Guatemala—and preceded Christianity. It was further explained that the Indians brought them from those countries during the sixteenth century when the invading Spaniards forced them to move to

California.

When a voice clearly announced, "This is Father Serra," Garland was astounded and wondered if his mind were playing tricks on him. He was also surprised that Serra spoke English, as one reference indicated he did not. Serra told him that the book was wrong and that there was only one language on his side. When Garland asked Serra if the photograph of him in Mrs. Parent's album was a true portrait of him, Serra confirmed that it was. He also identified other missionaries in the photo album as well as an Indian.

Serra told Garland that the crosses were of pagan origin and that the Indians buried them in ceremonies to appease their gods. He further stated that he prohibited such pagan worship but was unable to control the wild Indians.

At the direction of Serra and other "Invisibles" who spoke through the medium's megaphone, Garland and Williams traveled hundreds of miles through southern and central California and Mexico searching for more artifacts. They were often accompanied by relatives or friends to help them in the search and in the digging. The spirits would tell them where to go, where to stop, which direction to walk, and then where to dig. They found sixteen artifacts, similar in substance and design to those collected by the Parents, in ten widely separated locations. Some were in deep gullies, others high on cactus-covered hills far from the highway. One was hidden in a ledge of sandstone behind a wall of cactus plants which Garland had to chop away before finding it. For the skeptic who might have claimed that Williams went all over the state planting the artifacts for Garland to find, Garland wrote that this would have been an impossible task. Moreover, it was clear that the grounds covering the artifacts, some buried more than two-feet deep, had not been disturbed for many years. It was equally clear that Williams had neither the time nor the motive to carry out such a hoax.

Garland had ended his 1936 book still a little skeptical when it came to psychic phenomena, although his skepticism had to do more with whether it was proof of life after death rather than whether it was supernatural. Although he could not bring himself to state it in so many words, he appears to have finished his 1939 book on the buried crosses as a believer in life after death. How many readers of his book were convinced is unknown. The story probably exceeded the "boggle threshold" of the average reader and was looked upon as nothing more than a work of science fiction.

As for the crosses and other artifacts, twelve of the sixteen found by Garland are now on display at the West Salem Historical Society Museum. It is unknown what happened to the other four. The original 1,500 or so were apparently donated by Garland to the Museum of the American West in Los Angeles in 1939, but they are no longer in the museum's inventory. Perhaps they are now "buried" in someone's basement or making their way around the California flea markets.

Eighteen

The Mystery of Patience Worth

[Patience Worth] must be regarded as the outstanding phenomena of our age, and I cannot help thinking of all time."
   —**W. T. Allison,** Professor of English Lit., Univ. of Manitoba

"Many moons ago I lived. Again I come—Patience Worth my name" (Prince 1964).

So began the communication coming from the Ouija board being played with on July 8, 1913, by three St. Louis, Missouri, women. Patience Worth would later identify herself as the spirit of a seventeenth-century English woman who had migrated to the United States, where she was killed by Indians at age forty-four or forty-five.

Over the next twenty-four years, Patience Worth dictated approximately four million words, including seven books, some short stories, several plays, thousands of poems, and countless epigrams and aphorisms. She would be acclaimed a literary genius, her works compared with Shakespeare, Chaucer, and Spenser. She was called a wit, a poet, a dramatist, and a philosopher. "The unusual distinction about this Patience Worth is her exceptional and consistent intelligence," a *New York Evening Sun* review read. "She shows in all her messages every sign of a vigorous, keen mentality" (Prince 1964).

Of her book, *Hope Trueblood*, a reviewer for *Lady's Pictorial* of London offered: "…it will stand as a landmark of fiction by a new writer, who will take a prominent place among great writers" (Prince 1964).

From the *Chicago Mail*: "You will wonder at the sheer beauty of the story's thought and diction. You will be convinced that here is a tale from the pen of a master word builder" (Prince 1964).

A *New York Tribune* review of *Hope Trueblood* read: "The psychological analysis and invention of the occult, the dramatic power displayed in the narrative are extraordinary, and stamp it as a work approximating absolute genius" (Prince 1964).

The three St. Louis women—Pearl Curran, Emily Hutchings, and Mary Pollard—had begun experimenting with the Ouija board a year earlier. It was something by which to pass the time while Curran's and Hutchings's husbands played pinochle in another room. Curran and Hutchings would keep their fingertips on the planchette, while Pollard, Curran's widowed mother, would record the messages letter-by-letter. For the first few months, little more than gibberish came through, but then Curran's father and Hutchings's mother supposedly communicated with trite messages. Curran eventually became bored and frustrated with the "spiritualistic nonsense," but Hutchings, who had encouraged the game in the first place, persuaded her to continue. Then, on that warm July evening, Patience Worth made herself known.

"About me you would know much," Patience responded when the women asked her to further identify herself following her introduction. "Yesterday is dead. Let thy mind rest as to the past" (Prince 1964). When Hutchings asked Patience if she had been married, Patience replied, "Ye gods! Let bygones be bygones" (Prince 1964).

When Pollard commented that Patience's reluctance to talk about herself was possibly the result of not having a respectable past, Patience responded with anger: "Wilt thou but stay thy tung! On rock-ribbed shores beat wisdom's waves. Why speak for me? My tung was loosed when thine was yet to be" (Prince 1964).

However, the women persisted in wanting to know more about their new contact from the "Other Side." Patience provided them with the information on her English background and her tragic death, mentioning that she had lived from 1649 to 1694. With much bantering and more sarcasm, Patience made it clear that she was there to provide some wisdom, not to talk about herself. Over the next several months, Patience Worth dictated a number of poems and epigrams but further rejected requests by the three women for background information on herself as well as their requests for more universal truths. Reacting to the frustration of the three women, Patience responded: "Beat the hound and lose the hare" (Prince 1964).

On October 17, 1913, the three women took their board to the home of Mr. and Mrs. Fred Arnold. When Mr. Arnold demanded that Patience reveal some secrets of her world, she replied: "Thou wouldst untie the knot tied by the Master Hand." When Arnold persisted, Patience relented slightly, dictating: "Believe me, good souls, life is there as here" (Prince 1964).

Until March 1, 1914, it was assumed that both Curran and Hutchings had to be present for Patience to communicate. But, on that date, John Curran, who initially scoffed at the parlor game, sat at the board with his wife. Messages from Patience came through. Attempts by Hutchings to channel Patience without Curran were unproductive, and Hutchings would soon become a mere observer as other social friends sat with Pearl Curran at the board. Eventually, Curran found that she did not need the board at all. She would take dictation from Patience with a pencil, a process known as automatic writing, and later by using a typewriter. At times, Curran would engage in conversation with researchers and other observers as her hands continued receiving words from Patience.

Called by Patience Worth her "harp," Pearl Curran was a thirty-year-old housewife who had, following a nervous breakdown, dropped out of school at age thirteen. Inspired by her mother's love of music, she became a piano and voice teacher until, at age twenty-four, she married John Curran, a businessman twelve years her senior. Curran's limited education and travel were totally inconsistent with theories of conscious fraud or subconscious memories. Even English scholars struggled with some of the archaic Anglo-Saxon language. In one of her novels, Patience dictated, "I wot he fetcheth in daub-smeared smock." Even in the early 1900s, the word "fetch" was rarely used, but when used it meant to "go and get" someone or something. Patience used it as synonymous with "came" or "cometh," which philologists confirmed as the word's original meaning.

W. T. Allison, professor of English literature at the University of Manitoba, observed that Patience Worth dictated words found only in Milton's time and some of them had no meaning until researched in dialectic dictionaries and old books. Allison, who visited the Currans, reported that in one evening fifteen poems were produced in an hour and fifteen minutes, an average of five minutes for each poem. "All were poured out with a speed that Tennyson or Browning could never have hoped to equal, and some of the fifteen lyrics are so good that either of those great poets might be proud to have written them," Allison offered (Prince 1964).

When a philologist asked Patience how and why she used the language of so many different periods, she responded: "I do plod a twist of a path and it hath run from then till now" (Prince 1964). When asked to explain how she could dictate responses without a pause, she replied: "Ye see, man setteth up his cup and fillet it, but I be as the stream" (Prince 1964).

The mystery of Patience Worth became public on February 7, 1915, in a feature article appearing in the *St. Louis Globe-Democrat* by Casper S. Yost, the Sunday editor of the newspaper. Yost, who later founded the American Society of Newspaper Editors and served as its president from 1922 to 26, had attended a Ouija-board session on October 16, 1914 and then made repeated visits before writing his story, which appeared as a five-part series in the Sunday paper. Yost said that he had known the people involved for many years and was certain that they were not charlatans. He wrote that the

Pearl Curran.

intellect of Patience Worth justified any man's respect, referring to it as "keen, swift, subtle, and profound."

Yost's articles caught the attention of William Marion Reedy, the editor of *Reedy's Mirror*, a highly-regarded literary journal with an international circulation. While Reedy conceded that the poems of Patience Worth were "extraordinary" and "near great," he at first concluded that someone with a special literary interest in older English poetry was guilty of a hoax. When Reedy was invited to attend one of Curran's sessions, he accepted with some reluctance, later commenting that he had felt it would be a waste of time. However, upon observing the phenomenon, Reedy was immediately intrigued. He would sit with Curran through a number of sessions and carry on a dialogue with Patience Worth.

In the *Mirror* of October 1, 1915, Reedy told the world of his "flirtation" with Patience Worth. He explained that he had ruled out "fakery" and stated that he had absolutely no question as to the integrity of the parties involved. He further noted that Curran did not always understand his questions or the responses by Patience Worth. He called the spiritual content of Patience's poetry "an archaic Wordsworthianism, with a somewhat of Emersonism" (Prince 1964). He described her as piquant in the extreme, witty and aphoristic in a homely way, and saucy but never rude. "She will not answer personal questions about herself or tell you the usual stock things of so many spirit communications," he wrote, "about lost jack-knives in the distant past, or when your wealthy grandmother is going to die… None of that stuff goes with Patience…She is ready with repartee and she says things that probe the character of her questioners" (Prince 1964).

But Reedy rejected the idea that Patience Worth was a spirit, stating that he simply could not believe it possible for the dead to talk to the living. He considered the secondary personality theory, and even asked Patience if she and Mrs. Curran were the same entity. This theory, Reedy concluded, would be no less mysterious than the spirits theory. Patience immediately lashed out at the suggestion that she was a secondary personality of Pearl

Curran. "She be but she and I be me," Patience ended her discourse on the subject (Prince 1964).

Patience Worth was becoming an international celebrity. The mystery deepened with the completion of her first books, *Red Wing*, a six-act medieval play, and *Telka*, a medieval drama of some sixty thousand words. The latter was completed with seven thousand words in two sittings of three hours each. As Casper Yost saw it, *Telka* was a literary composition quite beyond the probable conception or execution of a finite mind. He concluded that this work proved the independence and separateness of Patience's personality.

Patience's most celebrated work, *The Sorry Tale*, a 644-page, 325,000-word novel about the last days of Jesus, was released in June 1917. As Yost, who was present when much of the book was dictated, explained, the story was begun without any previous knowledge on the part of Pearl Curran of the time and conditions of Palestine beyond what is revealed in the New Testament. Yet, the story goes far beyond what might be gleaned from the New Testament. "In one evening, 5,000 words were dictated, covering the account of the crucifixion," Yost reported in the preface of the book. "At all times, however, it came with great rapidity, taxing the chirographic speed of Mr. Curran to the utmost to put it down in abbreviated longhand. The nature of the language made it unsafe to attempt to record it stenographically" (Prince 1964).

In its review of the book, *The National* wondered how the mysterious story-teller became familiar with the scent and sound and color and innumerable properties of Oriental marketplaces and wildernesses, of Roman palaces and halls of justice. The *New York Globe* stated that it "exceeded *Ben Hur* and *Quo Vadis* as a quaint realistic narrative." The Columbus (Ohio) *Dispatch* opined that no other book gaves one so clear a view of customs, manners, and character of the peoples of the time and place.

Patience Worth continued to dictate until Thanksgiving Day, 1937, when Pearl Curran caught a cold. Pneumonia developed and she died nine days later. During nearly a quarter of a century of dictation, Patience Worth was investigated by numerous scholars and scientists. Many of them leaned toward the subconscious theory, but Dr. Walter Franklin Prince, who investigated for the American Society for Psychical Research, summed it up this way: "Either our concept of what we call the subconscious must be radically altered, so as to include potencies of which we hitherto have had no knowledge, or else some cause operating through but not originating in the subconsciousness of Mrs. Curran must be acknowledged" (Prince 1964).

All agreed that there was much truth and wisdom in Patience's words, but academia continues to struggle with the simplest of words uttered by Patience Worth: "She be but she and I be me."

The Wisdom of Patience Worth

Patience Worth was often asked to comment on various subjects. Here is a sampling of her responses:

On what is God: "If I were with one word to swing HIM, that word would shatter into less than the atoms of the mists that cling the mountain tops. If I should speak HIM in a song, the song would slay me! And going forth, man would become deaf when he listed. If I should announce HIM with a quill and fluid, lo, the script would be nothing less than Eternity to hold the word I would write."

On how man is to know God: "Alawk! Thy heart is packed afull o' Him, brother. Aye, and thou knowest. Then speak so, and say tis well, for sure as sun shall rise, thy dust shall rise and blow unto new fields of new days. Thou hast walled up thy heart o' words and yet it showeth although the patches o' thy words."

On death: "Cheap pence paid for eternity and yet man whines!"

On life: "Life is a gaysome trickster. Yea, life poureth about the atoms o' man wines of cunning, and equally is he filled up of Him. Thereby is man given freely and his lighting unto life leaveth him for his choosing. Aye, and the giving be wry-fallen atimes, for flesh to tarry long and dance with life, fearing the greater thing athin it."

On philosophy: "Philosophy is a bony nag and her gait is woeful. He who rides must spur her well with his ain imagination."

On hope: "The seine each man flings to the water of the day, and ah, the motley catch!

"And yet, and yet each morrow men do cast and cast, and e'er shall cast and cast and cast."

On laughter: "Me thinks that of all the gifts from Thy prolific hand, laughter, next to love, is dearest."

On learning: "Wisdom scratcheth the itch of the lout, while learning searchest for the flea."

On fear: "The undergarment of every armor. Man moutheth over words, and hangeth his wisdom with garments of words. Man knoweth certainties which even God doubteth."

On the press: "The gab wench of the day!"

On the women of her day: "Chattels; beasties, verily. Ye should have seen me mither's thumb—flat with the twistin' o' flax, and me in buskins, alookin' at the castle, and dreaming dreams!

On the Flappers of the 20s: "They dare what the past hoped for."

On New York: "A gaudy bubble paused, reflecting the motley day;

"A tenuous thing, a magic thing, the culmination

"Of man's desire, the pinnacle of his attainment, --

"A gaudy bubble."

On London: "Well, I'm sayin' you, tis a sogged puddin',

"Heavy o' wit, smug in honor, yea, honorable withage."

On Goethe: "What a song—and what an understanding!

"What harmony, what magic trick was his!

"Behold! he hath made his tongue holy

"Through his use in utterance of it!"

On Abraham Lincoln: "Behold, how humility, faith, and simplicity write with sure hand a luminous script pon the page of the day!"

On the doctors of her day: "A sorry lot, eh? Aye, and they did for to seek of root and herb;—aye, and play pon the wit, or the lackin' o' it!"

On scientific fundamentalism: "Man's law is precision, God's is chaotic. Man's wisdom is offensive to God, therefore He shows his displeasure in complications. To man the complications are chaos, thereby is man deceived. To God, man's precision is the fretfulness of a babe, aye, and man at his willful deceiving is undone. Then to God, man is precisively chaotic; to man, God is the disruption of precision."

Nineteen

Dead Monks Assist in Uncovering Abbey

They are not to be accepted with credulity, but are subjects for critical analysis, and must be weighed and examined, with all the rest, in the light of reason, assisted by every useful means of normal research and exploration.

—Frederick Bligh Bond (on the Glastonbury Scripts)

On June 16, 1908, Capt. John Allen Bartlett, a retired military officer living in Bristol, England, took a pencil in hand. Frederick Bligh Bond, a Bristol architect and archaeologist, sat at a table with him, holding firmly the foolscap paper below the pencil. As recorded in The *Gate of Remembrance*, authored by Bond and published in 1918, the following words flowed from the pencil: "Digge east beyond the beds of feathered grasses. There was a passage to the east doore in ye walle to the streete. In the midst it remaineth. There was a lodging where now is the great howse, and wee loved passages. They were safe, and the priesthood loveth secret places. There is somewhat in us that loveth mystical things, so we tell not all, but leave it to the love which seeketh and is not wearied" (Bond 1918).

This was part of one of more than sixty messages now referred to as the "Glastonbury Scripts," supposedly communicated by long-dead monks who had once lived at Glastonbury Abbey in southwest England. Bond had been commissioned by the Church of England to excavate the abbey ruins and had solicited the help of Bartlett, an amateur automatist, or medium, capable of producing what is called "automatic writing." Possibly, because he was concerned about having his name associated with such "occult" practices, Bartlett used the pen name of John Alleyne.

Some of the messages, especially the early ones, came through in Latin. Most were in Old English, but some were mixed Latin and Old English, described by Dr. Ralph Adams Cram, who wrote the preface to Bond's second book on the phenomena, *The Hill of Vision*, as "corrupt and colloquial *monk Latin*." As is usually the case in automatic writing, punctuation marks were absent, and were added for clarity. Bond would often put a question to the spirits and wait for an answer. At times, the communication would stop abruptly and begin again with a different influence or handwriting. Sketches of buildings would sometimes accompany the writing.

On December 5, 1908, after Bond had asked for clarification on a prior message, the following came from Bartlett's pencil, apparently a case in which one communicating spirit attempted to interpret for another: "Awfwold ye Saxon hath tried, but hee knows not ye tongue. He hath somewhat of olden tyme that ye have found in ye este [quest?]. He sayth hee hadde a house or housen in wattlework and a church within the forte, ye which wee did enter when wee made Edgar hys newe chappell. So he sayeth" (Bond 1918).

The most frequent communicator and usual "spokesman" identified himself as Johannes Bryant, aka Johannes de Glaston, a monk and stonemason who said he had lived from 1497 to 1533. He described himself as a fat, cheery man who preferred fishing to his regular duties. On December 9, 1912, Johannes, responding to a question by Bond about a staircase in one of the abbey buildings, stated: "Soe I remember those stayres for my fatness. But it availed me not, tho' my father Prior recommended it oft. Alas!

I waxed more fat. Not that my belly was my god. I wot not! But I was cheery and troubled not, save for services in ecclesia, for better loved I the lanes and the woods where walked I much—with weariness because of my weight. So said I, 'It is the Lord's will. Somme be made fat, and somme be lean'; and this I said to they that jibed, that the gates of Heaven are made full wide for all sorts, so that none created should stick within the portal. This I said, for they vexed me with their quips" (Bond 1918).

At times, other monks seemed to question the information provided by Johannes. In the fourth sitting, during 1907, Johannes was apparently rudely interrupted by another monk, as the following message came through: "Gulielmus de Glaston shall speke…Johannes would speke of hys tyme. The older tyme wasne know to hym. My punishment is past, but Johannes is yet in pain" (Bond 1918).

On March 17, 1908, after Bond had asked for someone from an earlier era to fill him in on the location of altar stones that were set down many centuries before Johannes, an unidentified communicator wrote: "What wold they tell ye? Their works were rude, and have departed. The abbey is not of them—nothing save certain books…We who speke are of its different orders: Gulielumus of old tyme, and Johannes later, and he who builded last—our Abbot Beere. What more is needed? We point the way; to you it is to follow, and all that is needed is given you. Worke with brain and handes, and all is there. We worked in our day: ye must work in yours. Ne work, ne wages—ne what you call honour" (Bond 1918).

The abbey ruins are situated on thirty-seven acres of land in the center of the market town of Glastonbury, about 140 miles southwest of London and thirteen miles inland from the Bristol Channel in what is called the West Country, on the plains of Somerset County. References on Glastonbury are vague as to the actual establishment of the abbey. This is because Christian tradition represented by the abbey evolved over many years while retaining some of the Druidic and Celtic Church influences that preceded it. It is said that Joseph of Arimathea, the great-uncle of Jesus of Nazareth, came to Glastonbury in A.D. 63, accompanied by eleven companions, at the direction of St. Philip the Apostle, to convert the pagans. Aviragus, the king at that time, gave the twelve men the Island of Ynys-witrin (Glastonbury), where they built a church called the *vetusta ecclesia* in honor of the Blessed Virgin Mary. Legend has it that Joseph brought with him the Holy Grail, the chalice used by Jesus at the Last Supper, and that he buried it at the foot of the Tor, at a place now known as the Chalice Well.

St. Patrick is said to have come to Glastonbury in 433, teaching the hermits there to live together as cenobites, then becoming their abbot and remaining in Glastonbury until his death, when his body was buried in the *vetusta ecclesia*.After St. Patrick's death, St. Benignus, his disciple, became the abbot and also died there.

The monastery at Glastonbury was founded in A.D. 601 when Gwrgan Varvtrwch, King of Dumonia, gave the land to the Celtic Church, which was under the direction of Abbot Worgret. The monastery was ravaged by the Danes in 878, although the *vestusta ecclesia*, also referred to in later years as the Old Wattle Church, was not destroyed. St. Dunstan is credited with restoring the monastery to greatness after becoming its abbot in 943 and placing it under Benedectine rule.

In 1184, a fire destroyed the Old Wattle Church and the greater part of the Benedictine Monastery. The present visible ruins date back to 1186, when Bishop Reginald dedicated the Chapel of the Blessed Virgin on the west end of the grounds and the foundation for the ecclesia major, the primary remains of today.

After King Henry VIII broke with Rome and declared himself head of the Church of England, he ordered that monasteries and abbeys be dissolved. The Glastonbury Abbey was plundered in 1539. Most of its stones were later carried off for construction of roads, quarries, and cottages, and gradually many of the foundations were covered and disappeared from sight, some a full six feet under ground. "The abbey did not languish and die from internal corruption," wrote Dion Fortune. "It fell as a great ship founders, at one

Arch at Glastonbury.

moment going on its way, at the next plunging to destruction with all hands" (Fortune 1986).

Soon after its destruction, the abbey grounds fell into private hands. It was not until 1908 that the Church of England took ownership, although in anticipation of acquiring the property plans were being made in 1903––04 to preserve it. Bligh Bond, a Fellow of the Royal Institute of British Architects and a member of the Somersetshire Archaeological and Natural History Society, was appointed Director of Excavations at Glastonbury. This was a non-paying, seasonal job, one which Bond, who specialized in ecclesiastical architecture, took on as something of a hobby while he continued his regular architectural practice in Bristol.

Bond had available to him various antiquarian works, the most important of which was *Architectural History* by Professor R. Willis, published in 1866. However, while the references mentioned Edgar Chapel and Loretto Chapel, the locations of these two chapels were not specified and remained a mystery when Bond undertook his work.

Born in 1864, Bond had developed an interest in psychic matters well before being appointed to head up the Glastonbury dig. He was a member of the Society for Psychical Research, an organization whose membership included a number of esteemed British scientists, such as Sir Oliver Lodge, Sir William Barrett, and Sir William Crookes. Apparently, it was through this organization that Bond befriended Bartlett and began experimenting with automatic writing. Initially, neither Bond nor Bartlett accepted the popular hypothesis that the phenomenon is the result of discarnates controlling the nervous system of the medium. They looked upon it as a tapping into some universal memory or cosmic consciousness. Because the communicators had displayed distinct personalities, Bond would later change his mind and accept the spirit hypothesis.

It was on November 7, 1907, that Bond and Bartlett first began experimenting with automatic writing relative to Glastonbury Abbey. It is not clear from Bond's book, but indications are that they had had positive results on other subjects before that date. "Can you tell us anything about Glaston-bury?" Bond put the question to an unseen communicator, or, as he appar-ently then understood it, to the universe (Bond 1918). Bond would place two fingers on the back of Bartlett's hand, a method often employed in auto-matic writing to add whatever psychic power a "sitter" might have to that of the medium's power. While waiting for an answer, the two men would remain passive and talk casually on other matters. In clear, eloquent Eng-lish, the answer to Bond's question came back: "All knowledge is eternal and is available to mental sympathy" (Bond 1918). After a short interval, the fol-lowing flowed from the pencil: "I was not in sympathy with monks—I can-not find a monk yet" (Bond 1918).

Bond decided to ask a monk friend to attend the next sitting, hoping that it would establish a sympathetic link. It apparently worked as Bartlett's hand began drawing what Bond concluded was a fairly correct outline of the main features of the abbey church traced by a continuous single line. At the east end was a long rectangular addition, which was given a double line as though to emphasize it. Down the middle of the drawing there was a sig-nature—"*Gulielmus Monachus.*" A more detailed sketch followed, and the words "*linea bifurcata*" (bifurcated line) were written. Someone signing his name "*Rolf Monachus*" then began communicating in strict Latin, provid-ing some measurements relative to the Edgar Chapel (Bond 1918).

Subsequent sittings during November resulted in a hodgepodge of communication, some in English, some in Latin, some in monk Latin. Some were signed, some were not. Johannes Bryant emerged as the chief commu-nicator, speaking in monk Latin, but there was often a change of influence so that it was not always clear as to the identity of the communicator. As a group, the communicators referred to themselves as "The Watchers."

On November 13, the English-speaking communicator, apparently the "gatekeeper," began by stating that other influences were crossing his and that the monks were trying to make themselves felt by both Bartlett and Bond. Johannes then communicated and wrote: "Ye names of builded things are very hard in Latin tongue—transome, fanne, tracery, and the like…Wee wold speak in the Englyshe tongue" (Bond 1918).

When Johannes wrote that he was a lap mason, Bond asked what that was. Johannes replied that it was a "lapidator," or stonemason. When some conflicting information came through regarding dates of construction, Bond, on September 23, 1908, asked for clarification, and a spirit replied: "Wee know not your dates, nor the tymes gone by; but this we do know…" (Bond 1918).

Some of the measurements given to Bond proved to be exact to the inch. Others were off by several yards or more. One of the monks pointed out that it was difficult to give exact locations and measurements because there was overlapping construction over the centuries, one building on top of another, and the foundations rarely matched. The communications continued regularly over the next few months, sitting number 27 being on March 17. After that, they were less frequent, sitting number 61 on December 9, 1912, nearly five years later. Most of the communications had to do with the layout and construction of the abbey. The Edgar Chapel was quickly located by Bond based on information provided by the various monks. The Loretto Chapel was not located until 1919, following a long interruption in excavations due to World War I.

On at least two occasions, there is reference to "Arthur," apparently King Arthur. In sitting number 34, the following was communicated: "The tombe of Arthur in shining blacke stone was in front of ye altare. Ye can see hys size even now, an ye wis, in ye claye, and certain fragmentes that yet are for hym to seeke" (Bond 1918).

On January 26, 1912, Johannes seems to have been on the defensive after other monks pointed out his errors and commented that he had an idealized recollection of the abbey because of his strong attachment to it. They explained that he was earthbound by his love and that his spirit clung in his dreams to a vanished vision which his spirit eyes still saw. Seemingly suggesting a group soul or higher-self nature, Johannes, in his defense, responded: "Why cling I to that which is not? It is I, and it is not I, butt parte of me which dwelleth in the past and is bound to that which my carnal soul loved and called home these many years. Yet I, Johannes amm of many partes, and ye better parte doeth other things—*Laus, Laus Deo!*—only that part which remembreth clingeth like memory to what it seeth yet" (Bond 1918).

Rarely did Bond ask about matters other than the abbey, but on one occasion he, directly or indirectly, questioned something relating to reincarnation. A more fluent English-speaking spirit responded: "The facts live, and the emotions and events. The puppets die and are not. The leaf is reproduced; the ears grow; but the old time is dead. You understand not reincarnation, nor can we explain. What in you reincarnates, do you think? How can you find words? Blind gropers after immutable facts, which are not of your sphere of experience" (Bond 1918).

On several occasions the communicating spirits tried to make it clear that they did not have all the answers, while also pointing out that written records had been distorted. For example, on March 12, 1908, this message came through: "I, Galfrith, knew in my day. They who came spake in Latin, and not all knew the wisdom hid in the british tongue, nor eke the saxon. Some were wrote again, but the fathers were more sought than the Bards and much was heresay. What do ye long after, my son? The memory of man is but as the grass that fadeth, and they who would fain translate the word of the barbarian oft inserted what they desired but would not an they could. The hidden meaning they knew not which looked for the husk which covered it and soe much was lost for all tyme. The merlins spoke in what ye call an allegory, but the parable was what these fathers read, not the mystery" (Bond 1919).

For some ten years, Bond had kept his mystical sources a secret from the Church of England. It was shared with only a few friends, including Dr. Ralph Adams Cram, a fellow architect from the United States. In the preface to Bond's second book, *The Hill of Vision*, Cram stated that he met with Bond in 1912 and urged him to write out the whole story for publication and even offered to do it for him. But Bond rejected the idea, apparently realizing that it would meet with disfavor by the Church of England. Even though the foundation of orthodox Christianity had been built on such spirit communication, Church authorities, fearing that anything new might not be consistent with established dogma and doctrine, had closed the book on additional communications with completion of the Bible. Anything after that was branded as heresy, as "occult" messages inspired by the devil. Although Bond was a Christian, he believed he could "test the spirits" (1 John 4) or be "discerning of the spirits" (1 Corinthians 12:10) without church officials telling him which were good spirits and which were evil. "If a [message] be found true, it cannot be dictated by a spirit of falsehood; if sane, then not by insanity; if wholesome and moral, then not by a vicious or depraved intelligence," Bond wrote (Bond 1919).

Bond eventually changed his mind about writing a book, and *The Gate of Remembrance* was published in 1918. It invited contempt from the Church and scorn from fellow professionals. His reputation was further compromised after the publication of *The Hill of Vision* in 1919. That book rehashed some of the material in his first book, but went on to include automatic writing produced in sittings with several different mediums concerning World War I and other matters not pertaining to Glastonbury Abbey.

In an "attestation" letter to Bond's second book, Bartlett/Alleyne stated: "I am unable to recognize the resulting script as in any appreciable degree the reflection of any notions of my own, and although I am a wide general reader and possess a retentive memory, I find myself often curiously unable to retain a clear mental impression of these scripts after they have been read to me.It is by nature difficult for me to write a letter or to carry on a conversation in presence of any distracting influence such as music or talking by others. Yet during our sittings my attention is fully given to Mr. Bond's reading, and I feel my hand to be moved quite independently of my own volition. I have never seriously studied philosophy and have not followed the developments of modern theosophical thought. With Spiritualism I have had scant sympathy" (Bond 1919).

It was the beginning of the end for Bond. From 1918 until his death in 1945, "he was immersed in another kind of quest," wrote his biographer, William W. Kenawell, "an endeavor to prove to the Church, his architectural associates, his family, and his beloved Somerset Archaeological Society that he was neither a fraud nor partly insane" (Kenawell 1965.)

In early 1921, insult was added to injury when a co-director of excavations was appointed by the excavation committee. "For over a dozen years Glastonbury Abbey had been Bond's passion, his immediate and long-range concern, his very reason for living," wrote Kenawell. "But by now the Somerset Archaeological Society was thoroughly sickened and disgusted with the situation" (Kenawell 1965). In April 1922, Bond was relieved of his duties because of his refusal to work with the co-director.

As clients had been abandoning him since the publication of his first book, Bond was by this time in dire financial straits, a situation compounded by an earlier divorce and lengthy litigation concerning custody of the couple's daughter. He became editor of *Psychic Science*, a new quarterly publication. Following a lecture tour in the United States, he was persuaded to remain there and work with Cram in his architectural practice while also serving as educational director for the American Society for Psychical Research. Sometime around 1932, Bond was ordained a priest of the Old Catholic Church of America. Exactly what that entailed is not clear, but it apparently did not satisfy Bond, as he returned to England in January 1936, a defeated man. He lived his final years in rooming houses in North Wales, most of his time devoted to doing oil sketches of various churches.

While in the United States, Bond reestablished contact with Johannes through five other mediums, four of whom were unaware of the others and of Johannes. On May 17, 1934, the most humorous message from Johannes came through the automatic writing of Mrs. J. B. Stevens. Johannes said he wanted to confess his "great sin," committed while he was ferrying a row boat to abbey. He explained that a young woman came prancing up to the boat "like a young fawn" and beckoned him to wait. "She lept into the boat and said, 'My purse be the worse for a cent, and out threat mine ha'pence hath trollped. I'll kiss thee, laddie, to pay the score!' And the hussy kissed my hot cheek before I could say 'stop!' or say a prayer to St. Anthony. Its true I rubbed it off with the tail of my habit—but the memory remained and there is an unhold gladness that I could not rid myself of. I did penance by mopping the refectory floor on bended knees, yet glad was I for the kiss, and am to this day. Lord have mercy on mine o'er tainted soul!"

Bond died alone, apparently still believing in the imaginative function. "Give it truth to feed upon and it will evolve truth," he ended his first book. "And through the door of truth may enter that which will guide us to a wider knowledge."

How much the mysterious sources actually expedited the excavation is not clear. While Bond indicates that they were of significant help, skeptics argue that the ruins would have been uncovered sooner or later by orthodox archaeological methods and so there is no way to confirm Bond's story.

A visitor to the Glastonbury Abbey museum today will find only a passing reference to Bond and none to the Glastonbury Scripts.

Twenty

The Evangelist Who Discovered Spirits and Solved a Mystery

Of all the explanations conceivable, that one which attributes everything to imposture and trickery is unquestionably the most extraordinary and the least probable.

—**Maurice Maeterlinck** (1911 Nobel Prize winner)

As a young ordained Baptist minister, Charles S. Mundell had hoped to become another "Billy Sunday." "No evangelist ever preached total depravity, blood atonement, or eternal damnation with more passion or earnestness than I," Mundell wrote in *Our Joe*, published in 1922 (Mundell 1922).

As a fundamentalist, Mundell believed that mediumship was the work of the devil. Does not Deuteronomy 18:10–12 tell us that we should not consult the dead and Ecclesiastes 9:5 say that the dead know nothing? So what if 1 John 4:1 tells us to "test the spirits" and Corinthians 12:10 says that we should be "discerning" of the spirits. It's easier to condemn it than to open oneself to the possibility that old dogma and doctrine used to frighten the faithful and keep them in check might have been misinterpreted or mistranslated, perhaps just outdated.

"I was sincere!" Mundell continued. "I really believed these infamous dogmas, and believing them, considered myself Divinely called to preach them" (Mundell 1922). However, Mundell went on to explain that he gradually came to understand the error in his thinking, giving up evangelistic work and attending Pacific Unitarian School at Berkeley, California. before becoming a Congregational minister. In April 1920, he became pastor of the First Congregational Church in Jennings, Oklahoma, and then was transferred to Oklahoma City. But in spite of his more liberal faith, Mundell's bias against Spiritualism, or communication with the "dead," still remained. Yet, he read and was very much impressed with Sir Oliver Lodge's 1916 book, *Raymond or Life and Death*, in which Lodge, a renowned British physicist, reported on communicating with his son Raymond, who had been killed on the battlefield during World War I, through several mediums.

Something happened on August 7, 1921, that would completely change Mundell's bias. His twemty-one-year-old younger brother, Joe Mundell, was killed in a deer hunting accident in northern California. He had strayed from his party and was lost in the woods for several days before his body was found. There was speculation that he was distraught and had shot himself. There was also suspicion that he had been shot by other hunters and left to die. As the Mundell family was very close, the loss was felt deeply by all. Family members were particularly upset at the report that Joe had taken his own life. Charles and his wife left Oklahoma to be with the parents in Oakland, California., where they lived. Joe had also lived there, working for railroad at the West Oakland train yard.

On September 17, Charles, his wife, Margaret, and his mother, Verna, were sitting in the Mundell home in Oakland discussing Joe, life after death, Spiritualism, Lodge's book, and other aspects of psychical research when they decided to try some experiments in tabletipping, a somewhat crude form of mediumship in which spirits tip or tilt a table in response to questions put by those present. They opened with a prayer and then sat for about a half hour with no results. Charles was ready to call it a night when his mother asked that they wait a while longer. She had recalled reading books where sitters remained quiet for hours waiting for manifestations. Charles consented and about fifteen minutes later, the little stand table in front of them began "quivering and vibrating like something alive." Then, the table lifted off the floor several inches. Charles asked if a spirit was present and to signal "yes" by three tilts of the table and "no" by one tilt. The table tilted three times. Charles then told the invisible entity that he would slowly

Joe Mundell.

recite the alphabet and asked that a tilt of the table be given at the proper letter. After the tilting table spelled out H-A-R, Mundell asked if it was his Grandma Painter, Verna's mother, Harriet. Three tilts followed for "yes." After a few familiarization questions, Verna asked if Joe was with her. Three tilts of the table followed. Charles then asked if Joe could communicate. The table tilted only once, indicating "no." Margaret wondered out loud if perhaps Joe had not been over long enough to develop sufficient strength. The table then tilted three times.

Many other questions were asked and answered that night, primarily about other deceased family members, including two of Verna's children who had died in infancy. They were informed that both were with Grandma Painter.

On September 19, Charles called Mrs. Emma Nanning, a Spiritualist medium, to request a sitting. He went alone later that day, giving no name. No sooner had he entered when Mrs. Nanning said she saw the spirit of man enter the room with Charles. She then asked if he had a brother who had recently passed into the spirit world. Before Charles could answer, she told him that the spirit said he was his brother Joe, just recently passed, and that he was showing her an accident. "Tell mama I didn't do; it was an accident," the medium passed on Joe's words (Mundell 1922). Nanning went on to say that she was seeing Joe sitting down on a log with a gun in an area of mountains or hills. She added that Joe was attempting to make his way to a cabin a mile and a half or two miles from where his body was found. Charles was unaware of any cabin in the area but later verified that such a cabin existed, thus concluding that this was evidence the medium was not reading his mind.

Several days later, Verna and Margaret Mundell had a sitting with Nanning, not giving their names and giving no indication they were related to Charles. Nanning told Verna that her mother was standing in back of her. "She says, 'I have brought Joe to you!'" She then got the name Harriet for Verna's mother. Joe then came through and told his mother that he went quickly and that she should not grieve. "You are wiping out my spiritual life by your tears," he told her (Mundell 1922). Joe then explained the accident, which had still been a mystery. He said that he was in the process of rolling a cigarette when the gun fell and fired.

The following week, Charles and his father, Sam, attended a public sitting with Nanning and two other mediums. Sam's mother, Elizabeth, had died in Los Angeles a few weeks before, not long after Joe's death. Nanning came to Sam and told him that "Elizabeth comes to you. She says, 'I'm your mother. Everything here is so much different that I expected. I wasn't looking for this. It is all so strange. You must help me, my son. I can't understand it all—yet! I am groping for light'" (Mundell 1922).

Charles interpreted that to mean that his paternal grandmother (Grandma Mundell) was confused because, as a member of an orthodox church, she had expected golden streets, pearly gates, and jasper walls. Upon finding the spirit world no more than a continuation of this world, except pitched in a higher plane and of a more ethereal nature, she was having a difficult time getting her bearings.

On September 27, there was another table sitting at the Mundell home. This time, Margaret Mundell's father, Herman Brunke, came through. As he spoke limited English, Margaret put questions to him in German and answers were received accordingly.

Seeking even more communication, Charles, Margaret, and Verna took the ferry over to San Francisco the following day for a sitting at a public Spiritualist meeting with Mrs. Marie F. S. Wallace, whom they had never met or seen. About twenty other people were present. After giving what appeared to Charles to be accurate and satisfactory messages to others in the room, Mrs. Wallace came to Margaret and told her that her father had a message of love. To be sure she knew it was him, he asked her if she recalled the time he slapped her over the head with a newspaper. Margaret replied that she remembered the incident very well. Wallace also mentioned that he was showing her that he was killed in a fall from a high building after his foot struck something sharp, like a spike. While Margaret was aware that her father had fallen from a Chicago skyscraper, she was unaware of the spike or cause of the fall.

Wallace then came to Verna, telling her she heard a spirit calling, "Mama." She went on to relate the message: "I just sat down to rest. I was tired. I was leaning on a gun…It all happened so quickly, like a flash." Wallace then got the name, Joe. "Joe says, 'I still live.' He says something about black. 'Don't like for mama to wear black.' 'Please don't grieve for me. I am all right. When you grieve it makes it harder for me to get close to you—it makes aura so dense.' He says, 'Willie is here, too—and Annie!' (the Mundell children who died in infancy). Joe says, 'I made Charlie come home.' Joe also says, 'If Charlie hadn't come home, mama would have been here, too, by this time'" (Mundell 1922). Charles interpreted the latter comment to mean that Joe had impressed him to leave Oklahoma City and return to Oakland. He recalled the desire to return as "irresistible."

On October 2, Charles, Margaret, Sam, and Verna again attended a public meeting with Emma Nanning in Oakland. Nanning came to Margaret and told her "Vater" (German for "father") was present. He then gave his name as Herman. Charles took this as very evidential, especially since his wife looked more Spanish than German.

Two days later, the family again took the ferry to San Francisco for a private sitting with Mrs. Wallace. Wallace came to Sam Mundell and said she saw him as an official or leader of an organization having to do with railroads. In fact, he was general chairman of the railroad workers union. Wallace told him that he had fathered five children. Sam told her there were only four, forgetting that a fifth child died a few days after birth. Charles saw this as particularly evidential in ruling out telepathy.

Joe again came through, offering more evidential information and ending with the comment: "Papa, I can go where I please, and I don't have to wait for trains like you do" (Mundell 1922).

On October 12, Charles, Margaret, and Verna had another table sitting at the Mundell home. They waited about twenty minutes before the table tilted twice, indicating sprit presence. The alphabet was recited and the name H-a-r-r-i-e-t was spelled, again Verna's mother. Charles asked his grandmother how the tabletilting phenomenon worked. "It isn't any known law of earth," Harriet slowly spelled out. "It is spirit magnetism. I don't understand it, but I can use it. Just like electricity is used on earth. Raymond Lodge is experimenting on it in his father's laboratory. I am tired" (Mundell 1922).

Joe then communicated through the table. He was asked what it was like where he was and what he was doing. He replied that it was warm and bright with no fog or fleas. He was going to school and learning what he didn't have a chance to learn when he was a kid. He was then asked for more details on his accident. He explained that the gun was leaning against his leg as he rolled a cigarette. As he reached for a match, he knocked the rifle over. The next thing he knew he awoke in his grandmother's arms with Willie and Annie holding his hands. He felt no pain. He was now with many friends and loved ones.

The Mundells continued to search for other mediums. On October 30, they sat with Mrs. R. Hyams at the Trinity Spiritual Church in Oakland. She looked to Verna and said "…your son comes to you and gives the name of Joseph…He shows me that he passed out quite suddenly—in the mountains—beautiful mountains! He says, 'Mother, do not grieve for me. You are not only hurting yourself, but you are keeping me back from the progress I should otherwise make'" (Mundell 1922).

On November 7, Charles was in San Francisco on another matter when he decided to attend a public séance at the home of Mrs. M. J. Isles. About twenty other people were present. Isles was a trance medium controlled by a child-guide, Jewell. After giving messages to several others, the medium staggered in the direction of Charles, her eyes closed, throwing out her arms to him and crying with mingled joy and pain, "Charlie! Charlie! I'm Joe! I'm Joe!" After the medium threw her arms around Charles, the voice speaking through her told him to "give Mama my love." The medium then fell back in a dead faint. "I cannot believe that Mrs. Isles—whose personality seems to radiate sincerity and truth—could stoop to such a damnable, monstrous, hypocritical pretense," Charles wrote of the possibility she was a charlatan. "If the phenomena were not genuine, then God have mercy!" (Mundell 1922).

On November 16, Charles had a sitting with another medium, Mr. F. K. Brown of Oakland. Again, Joe communicated, stressing that his death was neither suicide nor murder, "just an accident." Charles continued to verify that it was actually Joe communicating. One very significant piece of information mentioned by Joe was the fact that Charles was wearing his old watch. When Joe mentioned that he (Joe) was still using the watch, Charles became confused and requested clarification. Joe explained that Charles only had the shell of the watch, but that he had the real watch. He further mentioned that he was using some of his old clothes, pointing out that the material might be in an old trunk in their mother's house but the "life of them" was with him on his side of the veil.

In all, Charles consulted five mediums. None of the mediums knew him or had his name on the first visit, seemingly ruling out fraud. In each case, Joe and other family members communicated. They also communicated at their home table-tilting sessions. It was more than enough to convince Charles that his brother Joe and other family members were still "alive." While Charles recognized the theory of mind reading, or telepathy, by the medium, he rejected that idea based on the personal nature of the communications as well as the fact that some of the information coming from the deceased relatives was not known to him or other living family members until they later checked on it. For example, no one knew about the cabin mentioned by Joe. And from whose mind would Joe's explanation of his accident have come? Could the medium, who knew nothing of Joe or the accident in the first place, have reached into Charles's mind, seen that his brother was in a hunting accident of some kind, and then created a story about his gun falling as he sat on a log and rolled a cigarette? That seemed pretty farfetched to Charles, who was inclined to accept the words of Maurice Maeterlinck, a philosopher and a Nobel Prize winner in literature: "Let us not accept some grotesque hypothesis rather than the simpler one of individual survival"(Mundell 1922).

Twenty-one

Earthbound Spirits

It is probable that the earthbound and the cranks can communicate more easily than can the more highly developed, and that they would be more persistent in their efforts.

—James. H. Hyslop, Ph.D.

It has been suggested by Bible scholars that the Old Testament prohibitions against communicating with the dead are misunderstood because what modern English versions now give as the word "dead" was in the original Aramaic and Hebrew the "spiritually dead," referring to low-level or earthbound spirits, those orthodoxy says are in "hell." Revelation coming to us through modern mediumship suggests that such earthbound spirits do exist and some of them are as evil and devious as they were in their earth lives. But not all of them are that way; some are simply bewildered or confused, apparently the result of not opening themselves to enlightenment while in the flesh. Dr. Carl A. Wickland, a psychiatrist and psychical researcher, dealt extensively with such spirits through the mediumship of his wife, Anna Wickland.

A member of the Chicago Medical Society, the American Association for the Advancement of Science, and director of the National Psychological Institute of Los Angeles, Dr. Wickland specialized in cases of schizophrenia, paranoia, depression, addiction, manic-depression, criminal behavior, and phobias of all kinds. In his 1924 book *Thirty Years Among the Dead*, Wickland stated that much mental illness was caused by intruding, or obsessing, spirits. "Spirit obsession is a fact—a perversion of a natural law—and is amply demonstrable," Wickland wrote. "This has been proven hundreds of times by causing the supposed insanity or aberration to be temporarily transferred from the victim to a psychic sensitive who is trained for the purpose, and by this method ascertain the cause of the psychosis to be an ignorant or mischievous spirit, whose identity may frequently be verified" (Wickland 1974).

Wickland recalled that as a young medical student at Cook County Hospital in Chicago in 1897 he had to dissect the leg of a male cadaver. Soon after he arrived home that evening, his wife staggered as though about to fall. She drew herself up and became entranced by a "foreign intelligence" who asked Wickland why he was cutting on his leg. When Wickland attempted to place his wife in a chair, the entity possessing her told him to get his hands off of "him." Being familiar with his wife's mediumship, Wickland recognized what was happening and explained to the entity that he had died and was controlling the body of his wife. The spirit apparently did not immediately comprehend and requested a chew of tobacco. Knowing that his wife abhorred the sight of chewing tobacco, Wickland concluded that her subconscious mind was not playing a part in the conversation. The entity then asked for a pipe, saying that he was dying for a smoke. After a lengthy discussion, Wickland was able to convince the entity that he had died and was possessing his wife. When the entity realized his true condition, he left. Wickland subsequently examined the teeth of the cadaver and found indications that he was a heavy tobacco user.

Not long after that incident, Wickland and some other students were assigned the dissection of a woman who had died seven months earlier. As

Wickland was working on the body, he was startled by a rustling sound coming from a crumpled newspaper on the floor nearby. A few days later, the Wicklands held a séance in their home. When his wife should have been coming out of her trance condition, Wickland observed that she was still "semi-comatose." As he attempted to check her, her entranced body rose suddenly and struck angrily at him, asking why he was trying to kill her. Wickland responded that he was not trying to kill anybody, but the entity possessing his wife, who gave her name as Minnie Morgan, said that he was cutting into her arm and neck. She further said that she struck the paper on the floor to frighten him, but he continued anyway. Wickland explained to her that she was already dead. After some time, she understood and left, promising to seek a higher life.

Another early experience involved Mrs. Wickland falling prostrate to the floor and entering a comatose state. After a long wait, an entity spoke through her, complaining that she had not taken enough carbolic acid. She gave her name as Mary Rose and said she lived at 202 South Green Street, Chicago, a street Wickland said he and his wife were entirely unaware of. Wickland realized that the woman had committed suicide but had not yet recognized that she had succeeded. He explained things to her, and her spiritual sight opened enough so that she dimly recognized the spirit figure of her grandmother, who had come to accompany her to the spirit world.

Upon investigation, Wickland found that a woman by the name given and living at the address given had been admitted to Cook County Hospital a week earlier and died the following day of carbolic acid poisoning. She apparently wandered about and was attracted to the Wicklands' home by the medium's "light."

After a number of such experiences, "higher intelligences" calling themselves "The Mercy Band" told Wickland through his entranced wife that they had found in Mrs. Wickland a suitable instrument for experimentation in helping victims of possession. As it was explained to Wickland, these earthbound entities become attracted to certain humans and attach themselves to the human aura, unwittingly conveying their thoughts to these individuals. The higher intelligences further explained that the earthbound spirits could not be helped by spirits on their side until they recognized they were "dead."

According to Wickland, his wife's mediumship was that of unconscious trance. Her eyes were closed and her own consciousness held in abeyance in a sleep state. She could remember nothing after coming out of trance. With Wickland's help, the higher intelligences would allow the ignorant spirits to temporarily possess Mrs. Wickland, without any injury to her, during which time Wickland would explain their condition to them and help them move on. The transfer of the spirits from the victim to Mrs. Wickland was carried out by static electricity being applied to the victim in the presence of Mrs. Wickland. According to Wickland, the electricity was harmless but effective, as the obsessing spirit could not long resist such electrical treatment.

In one case, Wickland said he conversed with 21 different spirits through his wife. In all, they spoke six different languages, while his wife spoke only English and Swedish. The majority of them were friends and relatives known to Wickland when they were alive.

From a patient referred to as "Mrs. A.," Wickland claims to have dislodged tirteen different spirits, seven of which were recognized by the patient's mother as relatives or friends known to her during their earth lives. One was a minister of their Methodist church, who had been killed in a train accident nine years earlier but was still unconscious of the fact that he was dead.

As Wickland learned, obsessing spirits sometimes purposely torment helpless humans and cause them to commit deeds of violence upon themselves. Moreover, the spirits of many with criminal minds during their earth tenure attempt to continue their former activities by controlling the bodies of mortals who are sensitive to their influence. One of Wickland's patients was a pharmacist who had become a drug addict, especially addicted to morphine. After the static electrical treatment was administered to the patient, the obsessing spirit jumped into Mrs. Wickland's entranced body and began coughing violently as the claw-like fingers of Mrs. Wickland's body were clutching about. Wickland asked what the problem was and the spirit replied that she was dying and needed some morphine. Wickland explained to her that she was already dead, but the spirit ignored his comments and continued to beg for morphine.

Wickland managed to calm her down enough to further explain the situation to her and ask her for a name. At first she couldn't remember, but after several moments of searching gave her name as Elizabeth Noble. She said that she was forty-two years old and was living in El Paso, Texas. After again begging for morphine, she noticed her husband, Frankie, standing there (in spirit). Frank Noble then took over Mrs. Wickland's body and explained to Wickland that he had died before his wife and had been trying to get her to realize she had "passed out," but had been unsuccessful. He thanked Wickland for explaining the situation to her and said that she would now understand and be better.

On April 4, 1923, a "Mrs. V." came to Wickland for treatment of her alcoholic condition. As soon as the obsessing spirit took hold of Mrs. Wickland, her body attempted to fight, commenting that "he" was just about to have a drink and have a good time when he was interrupted by Wickland. He complained of someone "pouring fire" all over him (the static electricity). He identified himself as Paul Hopkins and spoke of "Mrs. V." as his friend who frequently gave him good whiskey to drink. After a lengthy conversation, Wickland was able to convince Hopkins that he had died. Once he accepted that fact, he saw his mother, in spirit, there to help him adjust. Wickland recorded that "Mrs. V." had no further desire for alcohol after that.

According to Wickland, spirits who are ignorant of having "died" frequently hold on to their physical infirmities and continue to suffer pain. Such spirits can transfer their afflictions and pain to the person being possessed. He recalled the case of a patient, "Mrs. McA.," who was suffering intense pain in the head as well as many changeable moods. When the obsessing spirit was transferred to Mrs. Wickland, the spirit gave her name as Grace

Brusted, of Boston, but people were frequently calling her "Mrs. McA." and she was tired of being called that. She said she was too sick to talk with Wickland, but he managed to continue the conversation with her, explaining to her the fact that she had died. She replied that she could not take the pain any longer and was ready to die. After the way of progression was explained to her, the spirit's mother and grandmother appeared to her, and accompanied her away. After that, the patient was no longer bothered with headaches or moodiness.

On July 26, 1922, Minnie Morgan, the spirit whose cadaver was being dissected by Wickland back in 1897, returned to take control of Mrs. Wickland's body and speak to Wickland. She said she had come to thank Wickland for helping her. She explained that Minnie Morgan was no longer her name and that she had not yet advanced sufficiently to have earned a spirit name. However, she was happy and attempting to do good, step by step, by working with those in the slums, helping them to overcome their addictions, the same addictions she suffered from while in the flesh. "I wish I could take you along with me for a few moments to see the conditions in the lower sphere—what they call the earth sphere," she told Wickland. "Here is the sphere of whiskey, here is the sphere of morphine, here the sphere of the opium fiend, here the sphere of selfishness, and here the sphere of misers" (Wickland 1974).

Morgan went on to say that of all the conditions that of the miser is the worst. "He starves his mind because he wants money, money—and what is the result? In the earth sphere he is in the dark, but he sees money being spent and he is in hell. He suffers terribly."

As for murderers, Morgan said there were many degrees of murder, ranging from murder by quick temper to the cunning murderer, the one who plans and schemes out of greed. The latter, she said, can get into the magnetic aura of a human and control him to commit other murder and crimes. "The majority of murders and hold-ups are committed by spirits," she related. "They scheme and scheme, and use mortals as tools, until they wake up and realize what wrong they have been doing" (Wickland 1974).

Other psychiatrists apparently attempted to copy Wickland's success, but often misused the shock treatments and were unable to find sensitives, such as Anna Wickland, who could handle being possessed by earthbound spirits without ill aftereffects. The message, however, was clear—awaken to the spirit life while still in the flesh and live accordingly.

Twenty-two

Disaster "Survivors" Communicate

There are more things in heaven and earth, Horatio,
Than are dreamt of in your philosophy.

—Hamlet, Act i. sc. 5

"Pray for Hugh Lane."

That was the first message spelled out on the Ouija board being operated by Hester Travers Smith and Lennox Robinson in Dublin, Ireland, on the night of May 7, 1915. As was their usual practice, Travers Smith, the oldest daughter of Professor Edward Dowden, a Shakespearian scholar, and Robinson, a world-renowned Irish playwright, sat blindfolded at the board, their fingers lightly touching the board's "traveler," a triangular piece of wood which flies from letter to letter under the direction of a spirit control. They had experienced several controls over their years of operating the Ouija board, but on this particular night the control was a spirit known to them as Peter Rooney. Rooney would be in touch with others on his side and deliver their messages for them if they lacked the experience to communicate on their own. Reverend Savell Hicks sat at the table between Travers Smith and Robinson, copying the letters indicated by the traveler.

Following the prayer request, the traveler spelled out: "I am Hugh

Lane, all is dark" (Travers 1919). At that point, however, Travers Smith and Robinson were still blindfolded and had no idea as to the message. In fact, they were conversing on other matters as their hands moved rapidly. After several minutes, Hicks told Travers Smith and Robinson that it was Sir Hugh Lane coming through and that he told them he was aboard the *Lusitania* and had drowned.

On her way home that evening, Travers Smith had heard about the sinking of the passenger ship by German torpedoes, but she had not yet read the details, nor did she or the others know that Sir Hugh Lane was a passenger on the ship sailing from New York to England. In her 1919 book, *Voices from the Void*, Travers Smith states that she knew Lane and had heard that he had gone to New York, but it never occurred to her when she heard of the sinking that he was on board.

While distressed, they continued receiving messages from Lane, who told them that there was panic, the life boats were lowered, and the women went first. He went on to say that he was the last to get in an overcrowded life boat, fell over, and lost all memory until he "saw a light" at their sitting. To establish his identity, Lane gave Travers Smith an evidential message about the last time they had met and talked, although when Travers Smith asked for his cabin number on the ship as proof that it was Lane communicating, the number given to her was later discovered to be incorrect. She reasoned, however, that he was in a confused state and that it is not unusual for people to forget their cabin numbers. Nor is it unusual for boat passengers to remember where their cabin is located without memorizing the number.

"I did not suffer. I was drowned and felt nothing," Lane further communicated through Peter Rooney that night (Barrett 1918). He also gave intimate messages for friends of his in Dublin.

Lane, thirty-nine at the time of his death, was an art connoisseur and director of the National Gallery of Ireland in Dublin. He was transporting lead containers with paintings of Monet, Rembrandt, Rubens, and Titian, which were insured for four million dollars and were to be displayed at the

National Gallery. It was reported by survivors that Lane was seen on deck looking out to Ireland before going down to the dining saloon just before the torpedoes struck.

Lane continued to communicate at subsequent sittings. As plans were underway to erect a memorial gallery to him, he begged that Travers Smith let those behind the movement know that he did not want such a memorial. However, he was more concerned that a codicil to his will would be honored. He had left his private collection of art to the National Gallery in London, but the codicil stated that they should go to the National Gallery in Dublin. Because he had not signed the codicil, the London gallery was reluctant to give them up. "Those pictures must be secured for Dublin," Lane communicated on January 22, 1918, going on to say that he could not rest until they were (Travers 1919).

At a sitting that September, Sir William Barrett, the distinguished British physicist and psychical researcher, was present. Prior to the sitting, Travers Smith and Barrett discussed how evidential the messages from Lane were to them, although they could understand why the public doubted. After the sitting started, a man who said he had died in Sheffield communicated first. Then, Travers Smith recalled, Robinson's arm was seized and driven about so forcibly that the traveler fell off the table more than once. It was Lane, who was upset because of the doubts expressed relative to his communication.

W. B. Yeats, the famous poet, also reported contact with Lane, his close friend, through a medium in London. He said that the medium told him that a drowned man followed him into the room and then went on to describe a scene at the bottom of the sea.

Travers Smith recalled an earlier sitting, on April 15, 1912, when she and a "Miss D." sat at the Ouija board and received no results whatsoever. They had all but given up when they decided to wait a few more minutes. Then, a very rapid message came through the board, stating: "Ship sinking; all hands lost. William East overboard. Women and children weeping and wailing—sorrow, sorrow, sorrow" (Travers 1919). They had no idea what

the message meant and no more came through. Later that day they heard
that the Titanic had sunk. Travers Smith concluded that because of the rapidity of the message they got the last name wrong, as William Stead, a prominent British editor who was one of the victims of the disaster, communicated at subsequent sittings, telling about his death.

In fact, Stead, who had been on his way to New York to give a speech
on world peace at Carnegie Hall, began showing up at other places where
he could find the "light" of a medium. According to Rev. Charles L. Tweedale,
the Church of England vicar of Weston, Stead appeared at a sitting given by
Etta Wriedt, called by Sir Arthur Conan Doyle the best direct-voice medium
in the world, in New York on April 17. The plan was for Stead to accompany
Wriedt back to England on his return voyage so that she could demonstrate
her gift there. Wriedt made the trip without Stead and gave a sitting on May
6 in Wimbledon. In attendance were Vice-Admiral W. Usborne Moore and
Estelle Stead, Stead's daughter. Moore reported that Stead talked with his
daughter for at least forty minutes. He described it as the most painful but
most realistic and convincing conversation he had heard during his investigations of mediumship.

General Sir Alfred E. Turner reported that he held a small and private
sitting at his home with Mrs. Wriedt. "We had hardly commenced when a
voice, which apparently came from behind my right shoulder, exclaimed: 'I
am so happy to be with you again,' Turner reported. "The voice was unmistakably that of Stead, who immediately began to tell us the events of the dire
moments when the leviathan settled down. There was a short, sharp struggle to gain his breath and immediately afterwards he came to his senses in
another stage of existence" (Tweedale 1925). At a later sitting with Wriedt,
Turner saw Stead materialize, wearing his usual attire.

Tweedale also recorded that Stead was seen and heard on July 17, 1912,
at the home of Professor James Coates of Rothesay, a well-known author
and investigator, who had Mrs. Wriedt give a sitting with a number of witnesses. "Mr. Stead showed himself twice within a short time, the last appear-

ance being clearly defined, and none will readily forget the clear, ringing tones of his voice," Tweedale quoted Coates. "There in our own home, and in the presence of fourteen sane and thoughtful people, Mr. Stead has manifested and proved in his own person that the dead do return" (Tweedale 1925)

The *New York Times* of April 16, 1912, carried Stead's obituary, referring to him as an advocate of international peace and an investigator of psychical phenomena, as well as the author of *If Christ Came to Chicago* and the editor of the English *Review of Reviews* and of *The Pall Mall Gazette*. In a biography written by B. O. Flower, Stead is referred to as a cosmopolitan journalist with a rare blending of intellectual force with moral conviction, idealism with utilitarianism, a virile imagination, and a commonsense practicality that strove to make the vision a useful reality. Flower went on to say that Stead was a man of dauntless determination, superb moral courage, and untiring energy.

One survivor reported seeing Stead calmly sitting in the smoking room reading his Bible as other passengers scurried to the decks and the lifeboats. Another survivor recalled seeing Stead calmly holding back men who were attempting to board the lifeboats with the women and children. The same survivor also remembered Stead frequently discussing spiritual matters at meals.

In one of his many stories, *From the Old World to the New*, a novel published in 1892, Stead described the sinking of a ship called the *Majestic in the North Atlantic* from hitting an iceberg. The name of the ship's captain was Edward J. Smith, the same name as the captain of the *Titanic*. In an 1886 story for *The Pall Mall Gazette*, Stead wrote about the sinking of an ocean liner and how lives were lost because there were too few lifeboats. Whether these two separate stories were precognition on Stead's part or merely coincidence is not known, but Stead apparently did not foresee the tragedy when he booked passage on the *Titanic*.

While Stead may not have been fully conscious of his precognitive ability, he knew that he had mediumistic abilities as an automatic writer. In 1909, three years before his death, he published *Letters from Julia*, a series of messages purportedly coming to Stead from Julia T. Ames, an American newspaperwoman, for her friend Ellen, during 1892–93. Stead had met both women on his travels, and several months after Julia's death, Ellen told Stead about seeing apparitions of Julia in her bedroom. Having recently discovered that he had the gift of automatic writing, Stead told Ellen that he would see if she could communicate through him. "Sitting alone with a tranquil mind, I consciously placed my right hand, with the pen held in the ordinary way, at the disposal of Julia, and watched with keen and skeptical interest to see what it would write," Stead explained in the book's Introduction. "The bulk of the first series was written as letters from Julia to Ellen." (Stead, 1970)

When the *Titanic* went down, Estelle, Stead's daughter, was on a tour with her own Shakespearean Company. One of the members of the touring group was a young man named Pardoe Woodman. According to Estelle Stead, a few days before the disaster, Woodman told her over tea that there was to be a great disaster at sea and that an elderly man very close to her would be among the victims. In 1917, shortly after being discharged from the army, Woodman began receiving messages from William T. Stead by means of automatic writing. Estelle Stead then started sitting with Woodman and observing. She noted that the Woodman wrote with his eyes closed and that the writing was very much like her father's. Moreover, the writing would stop at times and go back to dot the "i's" and cross the "t's," a habit of her father's which she was sure Woodman knew nothing about.

Stead informed his daughter that there were hundreds of souls hovering over their floating bodies, some of them apparently not comprehending their new state as they complained about not being able to save all of their valuables. After what felt like a few minutes, they all seemed to rise vertically into the air at a terrific speed. "I cannot tell how long our journey lasted, nor how far from the earth we were when arrived, but it was a gloriously beautiful arrival," Stead recorded through Woodman's hand. "It was like walking from your own English winter gloom into the radiance of an Indian sky. There, all was brightness and beauty" (Stead 1970).

Upon arrival, the souls were welcomed by many old friends and relatives. From there, Stead was guided by his father and an old friend. Following an orientation tour, Stead was taken to a temporary rest house, one which resembled an earth place in appearance. The rest and adjustment period varied significantly, Stead reported, based apparently on one's beliefs and actions while in the body. He found that his adjustment was rapid, as nearly everything he had learned about the afterlife while in the body proved to be correct. Others continued to grieve and cling to their earth lives. "We are only a very little way from earth," he explained, "and consequently up to this time we have not thrown off earth ideas. We have gained some new ones, but have as yet discarded few or none. The process of discarding is a gradual one" (Stead 1970).

As for his initial attempts to communicate through other mediums, Stead said that there were souls on his side who had the power of sensing people (mediums) who could be used for communication. One such soul helped him find mediums and showed him how to make his presence known. It was explained to him that he had to visualize himself among the people in the flesh and imagine that he was standing there in the flesh with a strong light thrown upon himself. "Hold the visualization very deliberately and in detail, and keep it fixed upon my mind, that at that moment I was there and they were conscious of it" (Stead 1970).

He added that the people at one sitting were able to see only his face because he had seen himself as only a face. "I imagined the part they would recognize me by." It was in the same way he was able to get a message through. He stood by the most sensitive person there, concentrated his mind on a short sentence, and repeated it with much emphasis and deliberation until he could hear part of it spoken by the person.

Stead further explained that "judgment" is not made by a judge in wig and gown, but that every soul judges him or herself. He said that we have a full and clear remembrance of all our actions and that we are brought into a state of regret, happiness or unhappiness, despair or satisfaction accordingly.

"The mysteries of life are not revealed to you as a kind of welcoming gift on your arrival here," Stead went on. "You must not think that I, or any, have full knowledge on all subjects, profound or trivial, the moment we come to the spirit life…I cannot tell you when your grandson will next require new shoes…nor can I tell you the settlement of the Irish question. I can only see a little farther than you, and I do not by any means possess the key to the door of All Knowledge and All Truth." (Stead, 1970)

Stead stressed that "the presence or absence of contentment is entirely due to the earth life one has led, the character formed, opportunities taken and lost, the motive of and for your actions, the help given, the manner of use of help received, one's mental outlook and one's use and abuse of flesh power." (Stead, 1970)

"Letters" from Julia

In 1909, three years before his death resulting from the *Titanic* sinking, William T. Stead published *Letters from Julia*, a series of messages purportedly coming to him from Julia T. Ames, an American newspaperwoman, for her friend Ellen during 1892–93 by means of automatic writing. Here are a few of the messages:

On dying: "I did not feel any pain in 'dying.' I felt only a great calm and peace. Then I awoke and I was standing outside my old body in the room. There was no one there at first, just myself and my old body. At first I wondered I was so strangely well. Then I saw that I had passed over."

The soul after death: "When the soul leaves the body it remains exactly the same as when it was in the body; the soul, which is the only real self, and which uses the mind and the body as its instruments, no longer has the use or the need of the body. But it retains the mind, knowledge, experience, the habits of thought, the inclinations; they remain exactly as they were. Only it happens that the gradual decay of the fleshy envelope to some extent obscures and impairs the real self which is liberated by death."

On the afterlife: "There are degrees of Heaven. And the lowest heaven is higher than the most wonderful vision of its bliss that you ever had. There is nothing to which you can compare our constantly loving state in this world except the supreme beatitude of the lover who is perfectly satisfied with and perfectly enraptured with the one whom he loves."

On the Higher Self: "The Guardian Angel is indeed a kind of other self, a higher, purer, and more developed section of your own personality. This is perhaps a little difficult to understand, but it is true. There are, as well as good, evil angels, who are with us no less constantly, and they are also sometimes visible as Angels of Darkness when we come across…We are always swaying hither and thither towards our good and evil guides. We call them, or we did call them, impulses, wayward longings, aspirations, coming we know not where or whence. We see on this side where they come from."

On meeting Jesus: "I can only tell you that he is more than we ever imagined. He is the Source and Giver of all good gifts. All that we know of what is good, and sweet, and noble, and lovable are but faint reflections of the immensity of the glory that is His."

On judgment: "The thoughts and intents of the heart, the imaginations of the mind, these are the things by which we are judged; for it is they which make up and create, as it were, the real character of the inner self, which becomes visible after the leaving of the body."

Epilogue

The reader will likely ask why we don't hear such stories today. There are several theories as to why this is, the primary one being that mediumship is something that takes time and patience to develop. In those days before people were entertained by radio and television, it was not uncommon for them to socialize more and to experiment with such things as the Ouija board and séance circles as well as to spend more quiet time at home—time in which they could experiment with automatic writing and other forms of mediumship requiring a passive state. Consider the mediumship of Gladys Osborne Leonard, the subject of four chapters in this book. She and two friends had twenty-six unproductive development sessions before obtaining results. Then it took another eighteen months of development before Leonard became a proficient medium.

The story of Patience Worth, set forth in Chapter Eighteen, is also typical. It began in August 1912 when three bored St. Louis housewives decided to experiment with a Ouija board as their husbands played poker in an adjoining room. Except for a few words here and there, the women obtained no significant results for eleven months. Pearl Curran, one of the women, was very skeptical and wanted to move on to another game, but Emily Hutchings, who suggested the game in the first place, convinced her to stay with it a while longer. It wasn't until July 8, 1913, nearly a year after their first experiment, that the entity calling herself Patience Worth began communicating.

As it turned out, Curran, the skeptical one, was identified as the medium. Once her gift was recognized, it took many months for her to move from the Ouija board to more sophisticated methods of mediumship.

Hamlin Garland, a very skeptical psychical researcher whose research was discussed in Chapters Sixteen and Seventeen, reported on sitting silently in a darkened séance circle for as long as four hours before anything developed. Sophia Williams, one of the mediums investigated by Garland, wrote a book on the subject in 1946. In it, she states that she sat quietly each day for four years to learn the art of relaxation and complete detachment before her own mediumship began to really develop.

How many people today have that kind of patience? I certainly don't. I bought a Ouija board a few years ago and gave up after twenty minutes of no results. After reading books on automatic writing, another form of mediumship, I made several attempts to sit passively and wait for spirits to take over the pencil, but each time I gave up after about ten minutes. I think it's that way with most people. We want and expect immediate results.

There are other possible reasons, one of them being the moral atmosphere. Consider the amazing mediumship of Daniel Dunglas Home, as discussed in Chapter Three. Sir William Crookes, one of the world's leading scientists, had some twenty-nine meetings with Home with varying degrees of phenomena produced at all of them. However, the least phenomena were produced on May 28, 1873, Derby Day in England. According to Home, the gambling and drunkenness associated with Derby Day resulted in a negative moral atmosphere, one that prevented the higher spirits from communicating. Could the moral atmosphere in London in 1873 be any lower than it is worldwide now? Is it possible that today's materialistic, even hedonistic, world has created an atmosphere which the good spirits cannot penetrate?

A third possible reason may have to do with electrical interference. Many of the old mediums were informed by the spirits that lightning interfered with communication. Of course, electricity was in its infancy when the stories in this book took place. As to how electrical waves interfere, I have no idea. I am a journalist, not a scientist, although I doubt that there is any scientist living today who can explain it, especially since the majority of them reject the idea of spirit communication or even scoff at it. How can they understand something they don't believe in?

Still another possible reason for the decline in mediumship may be frustration on the part of the spirit communicators. It is clear from some of the stories in this book that the spirits have as difficult a time getting through to us as we do in getting through to them. Many of them pointed out that they were experimenting on their side of the veil as much as we were on our side. Seeing that their constant efforts in communicating with us were rejected by both mainstream science and orthodox religion, they may have decided that there was no further point in continuing with meaningful messages.

If you had the gift of mediumship and you began receiving messages from a spirit claiming to be a well-known person from the past, would you believe it was him or her, or would you suspect you were just imagining it? How would you know it was that person and not some earthbound spirit, an impostor, pretending to be that well-known person? If you were to convince yourself that it was the well-known person communicating, how many people do you think would believe you? What tests could you run to convince others that it was that person? Knowing what you were up against, why would such a person attempt to communicate in the first place?

What if the communicating spirit was simply a relative or friend whose name was unknown to the public? It's unlikely the rest of us would know about it as newspaper editors and book publishers are simply not interested in that type of thing today. They would look upon it as just another "ghost" story and make light of it.

All that is not to say that mediumship does not exist these days. There are still a few trance mediums and a number of good clairvoyant (seeing spirits) and clairaudient (hearing spirits) mediums today, although this type

of mediumship is hardly as dynamic as the trance, direct-voice, and materialization types that were ever present a hundred years ago. A few modern
clairvoyant/clairaudient mediums, such as John Edward, James van Praagh,
George Anderson, Sylvia Browne, and Colin Fry, have appeared on television programs in which they have demonstrated their gifts.

Dr. Gary Schwartz, professor of psychology, medicine, neurology, psy-
chiatry, and surgery at the University of Arizona, has been studying mediums in his Human Energy Systems Laboratory for several years and has concluded that they—at least some of them—are actually in touch with
discarnate friends and loved ones. "I can no longer ignore the data and dismiss the words," Schwartz, a former skeptic, wrote in his 2002 book, *The
Afterlife Experiments*. "They are as real as the sun, the trees, and our television sets, which seem to pull pictures out of the air."

When I interviewed Schwartz, who received his doctorate from Harvard and taught at Yale before moving on to the University of Arizona, for
several publications early in 2005, he spoke about the frustrations of dealing with closed-minded scientists. He had concluded that there is no experiment he could design to convince what he calls the super-skeptic of the
reality of mediumship. "The truth is that if you are absolutely convinced
that the phenomena can't be true, then no matter what experiment you
design, you can always find some way in which there might be fraud," he
told me. "Therefore, you are going to dismiss it or you're going to admit that
you got it in that case but you want to see it replicated by other people. Then
you want to see it replicated again, and it just goes on and on."

Schwartz also lamented the media coverage of his findings, pointing
out that reporters generally don't understand his research and distort the
facts. Clearly, most reporters treat the subject with a "tongue-in-cheek" slant,
as if not wanting to appear gullible.

In an interview with Dr. Jon Klimo, a San Francisco professor of parapsychology, I asked for his opinion as to why there has been such a decline
in quality mediumship. As he sees it, we operate within a politics of con-

sciousness involving conscious and unconscious contending of forces vying for the ongoing vote of our reality-created souls. "We all co-constitute the reality we are experiencing, and there is a lot of conditioning, propaganda, suppression, manipulation, and mind control involved," he explained. "The homeostasis-maintaining mechanism of the consensus reality and its locally severing mechanism seek to keep most of us on Earth at present from accessing the larger reality so the truth could set us free to ever more consciously move with and as part of God."

If I am interpreting that esoteric statement and Klimo's additional comments correctly, he is saying that there is a gradual "awakening" of consciousness taking place—an awakening that is being influenced by both positive and negative forces. He calls it a "war on the inner planes." The ability to accept the positive and reject the negative, thereby awakening to one's God consciousness, is an individual thing and is part of the challenge we face in our struggle to regain true consciousness, i.e., spiritual consciousness, something we somehow lost in what is symbolically depicted for us in the Garden of Eden story and called original sin.

From where I sit, the negative forces are winning the war and only when enough people begin pursuing spiritual paths will the tide turn. Some people are looking for God as a way out of this quagmire. They are taking the deductive approach, trying to find God before believing in a spirit world and an afterlife. It is much easier to take the inductive approach and find evidence of a spirit world and an afterlife, then letting God emerge from that. That is what prompted me to write this book, the hope that in examining these stories and pondering on them, some readers will be able to lift some of the veil and further awaken to their God consciousness.

Fortunately, even though the quality of mediumship does not seem to be what it once was, we have been given other phenomena, including near-death experiences and electronic voice phenomena, to help us go beyond blind faith. A more recent phenomenon is "induced after-death communication," as discovered by Dr. Allan Botkin, a psychologist who has been able to put grieving patients in touch with departed loved ones by means of EMDR (eye movement desensitization and reprocessing) therapy.

For those seeking spiritual truths, there is still much out there. But an understanding of mediumship as it was between 1850 and 1940 can serve as a solid foundation for finding the afterlife. I hope that I have been able to provide that foundation in this book.

Appendix A

Glossary

Automatic Writing: In this form of mediumship, the medium usually goes into a trance state and the communicating spirit then controls the medium's hand. Perhaps the most accomplished automatist of the twentieth century was Geraldine Cummins of Ireland. She would sit at a table, cover her eyes with her left hand on concentrate on "stillness." She would then fall into a light trance or dream state. Her hand would begin to write. Usually, her "control" (see "spirit control" below) would make some introductory remarks and announce that another entity was waiting to speak. Because of her semi-trance condition and also because of the speed at which the writing would come, it was necessary for an assistant to sit beside her and remove each sheet of paper as it was filled. It was also necessary for the assistant to quickly lift Cummins' hand to the top of the new page. In one sitting Cummins wrote two-thousand words in seventy-five minutes, whereas her normal compositions were laboriously put together, perhaps eight-hundred words in seven or eight hours. Beatrice Gibbes, her friend, stated that she witnessed the writing of about fifty different personalities, all claiming to be "dead," all differing in character and style, coming through Cummins's hand. (See also "Direct Writing" and "Inspirational Writing" below.)

   Channeling: Many messages coming through mediums are simple and mundane statements from recently passed friends and relatives. They are often evidential but rarely profound. Sometimes referred to as "spiraling" mediumship, channeling results in messages of wisdom and higher truths, purportedly coming from advanced spirits. It usually comes through automatic writing, sometimes from the trance voice. Some channeled messages are said to come from beings who have never been incarnate on the earth plane.

Clairvoyance: Derived from the French, meaning "clear seeing," this type of mediumship is often associated with **Clairaudience** ("clear hearing") and **Clairsentience** ("clear sensing"). While some mediums have all three abilities, others have only one or two. Clairvoyance is sometimes used in a very broad sense to include all forms of extra-sensory perception, including telepathy, precognition, and most types of mediumship. In the more limited sense, it refers to that type of mediumship not involving a significantly altered state of consciousness whereby the medium "sees" spirit forms and receives messages from them, often by pictures and symbols that must be interpreted by the medium. The mediumship often seen on television these days is of this type.

Direct Voice: This form of mediumship is sometimes confused with the "trance voice" type. In the latter, the communicating spirit takes over the speech mechanism of the medium, while in the direct voice the communicating spirit speaks independently of the medium's body, often through a levitating megaphone or trumpet. A trance state may or may not be required of the medium. It is said that the communicating spirit uses the ectoplasm (see below) of the medium to form something resembling a human larynx. The megaphone is required to amplify the spirit voice.

Direct Writing: This phenomenon should not be confused with automatic writing. In direct writing, the writing instrument is controlled by an invisible hand or by a luminous hand manufactured by the spirit from the medium's ectoplasm (see below). This phenomenon included what was often referred to as "slate writing" during the 1850 to 1900 era. In that phenomenon, a piece of chalk would be placed between two slates and spirit messages written on the slates.

Ectoplasm: This is a cold and clammy substance exuded by some mediums to permit spirit materialization. It is said to be vital energy or vitalized matter. Dr. Gustave Geley (1868–1924), professor of medicine at the University of Lyons, studied this phenomenon with the medium known as Eva C. He reported observing a cord of white substance proceed slowly from Eva's mouth down to her knees. It would contract, fold up, then expand and stretch out again. Geley saw a perfectly modeled hand materialize within the ectoplasm. He felt the hand and could feel the bones and fingers together with the nails before it vanished. Other spirits have fully materialized using the ectoplasm, as observed by Sir William Crookes in the famous Katie King case.

Inspirational Writing: The distinction between automatic writing and inspirational writing is not always clear cut. Generally, however, automatic writing involves some degree of trance, while in inspirational writing, the person is fully conscious. In Testimony of Light, Helen Greaves told how she received messages from her deceased friend Frances Banks. It was like taking dictation, as words, thoughts, and sentences tumbled out. Yet, she said, it was not automatic writing as she was perfectly in control. She wrote that she could feel Banks's mind using her mind.

Materialization: In this type of mediumship, spirits draw from the medium's ectoplasm and materialize all or part of their spirit body. Often, it is just a hand, but there have been a number of cases in which the full body materialized. The most famous of these cases was that of Katie King, as discussed briefly at the end of Chapter Three.

Ouija Board: This is a basic form of automatic writing (see above). The board has letters and numbers printed on it as well as "yes" and "no." The automatist's fingers rest on a triangular object known as the "traveler" or "planchette." The communicating spirit or "control" then guides the automatist's, or medium's, hands and the traveler to certain letters or numbers to spell out words and sentences. Often, two people will place their fingers on the traveler, giving more psychic power to it if both have mediumistic ability. Pearl Curran, the subject of Chapter Eighteen, began her experiments with the board with another person, but it was eventually realized that the power was coming through her and that no other person was necessary. Eventually, Curran could carry on a conversation with someone as her hand spelled out words on the board.

Rappings/Tappings: When the mediumship epidemic began in 1848 (see Introduction), the first messages came by this rudimentary method. Spirits would communicate by giving so many raps for each letter of the alphabet, slowly spelling out words and sentences, or would respond to a living person reciting the alphabet and then rapping or tapping when the person came to the proper letter. Or they would respond with so many taps for a "yes" and so many for a "no."

Spirit Control: Sometimes referred to as a "gatekeeper," "doorkeeper," or "guide," the control is a spirit who has learned to control or manage the medium from the "other side." When the medium goes into a trance, her spirit departs the body and the spirit control then takes over her body. The control then relays messages from other spirits, who are unable to use the medium's body. Often, the spirits are apparently lined up while waiting to communicate and it is also the control's function to maintain order so that the medium's body is not abused by them. It seems that spirits must achieve some sort of altered state of consciousness from their side in order to communicate with us, just as an altered state of consciousness is usually necessary for the medium on this side. Thus, the spirit control might be viewed as a medium on the other side. Occasionally, if a control feels that a particular spirit can achieve the altered state on their side without injuring the medium's body, the control will step aside and allow that spirit to use the medium's body. The scene in the movie Ghost in which Patrick Swayze, who had been murdered, takes over the body of Whoopi Goldberg, a medium, is not all Hollywood fantasy. Moreover, just as earthly mediums are not necessarily spiritually advanced humans, so we find that spirit controls are not necessarily advanced spirits. For example, Phinuit, an early control for Leonora Piper (see Chapters Seven through Ten), was considered a somewhat low-level spirit. He gradually gave way to George Pellew, a more advanced spirit, and Pellew eventually turned over management of Mrs. Piper to Rector and Imperator, both from even higher realms.

Table Tilting: This is another rudimentary method, similar to rappings and tappings (see above). The spirits would fully or partially levitate a table and provide messages by tilting or turning the table so many times for each letter of the alphabet, thereby spelling out words and sentences, or they would tilt the table at the proper letter when a person recited the alphabet.

Appendix B

Psychical Research Timeline

March 31, 1848—This day marks the beginning of paranormal phenomena at the home of the Fox family in Hydesville, New York. This leads to a mediumship "epidemic" in the United States and Europe.

January 1851—Judge John W. Edmonds, Chief Justice of the New York State Supreme Court, begins a two-year personal investigation of mediumship. Intending to debunk the phenomena, he instead becomes a dedicated Spiritualist.

1851—The "New York Circle," an association of prominent men and women, including Judge Edmonds, is formed to observe and report on spiritualistic phenomena. The group's first official meeting takes place on November 14, 1851.

1851—The Ghost Society is formed at Cambridge in England. One of the founders is Edward White Benson, later Archbishop of Canterbury. In 1853, Henry Sidgwick, Benson's cousin and later a founder of the Society for Psychical Research (SPR), joins the group. Seven years later, Professor Sidgwick becomes a tutor at Cambridge to Frederic W. H. Myers, a co-founder of the SPR.

1852—A Harvard University delegation, including poet William Cullen Bryant and Messrs. B. K. Bliss, William Edwards, and David Wells studies the physical mediumship of Daniel Dunglas Home, concluding that he is "a modern wonder."

1853—Dr. Robert Hare, a retired University of Pennsylvania chemistry professor and renowned inventor, begins investigating mediumship intent on showing it is all fraud. He comes to accept it as real and then becomes a medium himself. In 1855, he writes a book, *Experimental Investigation of the Spirit Manifestations.*

1853—French author Victor Hugo is exiled to the island of Jersey and begins an informal investigation of mediumship.

1854—French educator Hippolyte Leon Denizarth Rivail (Allan Kardec) begins an investigation of mediumship. In 1857, he publishes *The Spirits' Book*, which sets forth profound messages from the spirit world.

1860—American editor and statesman Robert Dale Owen writes *Footfalls on the Boundary of Another World*, discussing various psychic phenomena. Psychical researchers in the decades following would say that this book significantly influenced them in their decisions to investigate similar phenomena.

1866—Alfred Russel Wallace, co-originator with Charles Darwin of the natual selection theory of evolution, issues his first writing on Spiritualism, *The Scientific Aspect of the Supernatural.*

1869—The Dialectical Society of London appoints a committee, including biologist Alfred Russel Wallace, to investigate mediumship. The committee returns a report that the phenomena exist.

1870—Not satisfied with the committee's report, The Dialectical Society of London appoints renowned chemist William Crookes (later, Sir William) to investigate. On April 21, 1870, he has the first of many sittings with medium Daniel Dunglas Home. In 1872, he begins an investigation of medium Florence Cook. He reports that both Home and Cook are genuine mediums.

April 2, 1872—Rev. William Stainton Moses, an Anglican minister and English Master at University College, begins investigating mediumship, assuming it to be all trickery and fraud. He soon becomes a medium himself, receiving profound messages from a high spirit calling himself Imperator.

May 9, 1874—Two Cambridge scholars, Frederic W. H. Myers and Edmund Gurney, visit Rev. William Stainton Moses to observe his mediumship. They are fascinated and are encouraged to further explore the subject.

1875—Serjeant Cox, a lawyer who often sat with The Rev. W. Stainton Moses, organizes the Psychological Society of Great Britain. It is dissolved upon his death in 1879.

1876—Dr. William Barrett (later Sir William), professor of physics in the Royal College of Science at Dublin, submits a paper to the British Association for the Advancement of Science on the subject of mental telepathy, then called thought-transference. The Association rejects it. When Alfred Russel Wallace protests the rejection, Barrett is allowed to deliver his paper but not to publish it.

1879—The Cambridge Society for Psychical Research is formed to conduct investigation of mediums. It is a forerunner of the Society for Psychical Research.

1882—The Society for Psychical Research (SPR) is organized in London by eminent scholars and scientists, including William Barrett, Henry Sidgwick, Frederic W. H. Myers, and Edmund Gurney. Sidgwick becomes its first president.

1884—Professor Oliver Lodge (later, Sir Oliver), a physicist and educator, joins the SPR, interested primarily in telepathy while not believing in survival.

1884—Dr. Richard Hodgson, who had been teaching philosophy at Cambridge and law at University extension, is sent to India by the SPR to investigate Madame H. P. Blavatsky and the Theosophical Society. Hodgson submits a very controversial report that she is a fraud.

1885—Professor William James of Harvard University begins an investigation of the mediumship of Leonore Piper of Boston, Massachusetts, concluding that she is not a charlatan.

1886—A 1,300-page book titled *Phantasms of the Living*, authored by Edmund Gurney, Frederic W. H. Myers, and Frank Podmore is published. It strongly supports the telepathy hypothesis. It is Myers who gives the name "telepathy" to what was previously referred to as thought-transference.

1887—The American branch of the Society for Psychical Research (ASPR) is formed with Dr. Richard Hodgson accepting the position as its first executive secretary. William James turns over the investigation of Leonore Piper to Hodgson. Hodgson will dedicate himself to observing and studying her mediumship until his death in 1905.

1889—The SPR arranges for Leonore Piper to travel to England, where she is studied and tested by Frederic W. H. Myers and Professor Oliver Lodge. During the sittings with Lodge, Edmund Gurney, co-founder of the SPR who had died in 1888, communicates. Lodge and Myers come to accept the spirit hypothesis.

1891—The American Psychical Society of Boston is formed by disgruntled ASPR members who feel that Dr. Richard Hodgson is devoting too much time to Leonore Piper and not delegating research projects involving other mediums to qualified researchers. Rev. Minot J. Savage and B. O. Flower, an editor, are the founders, while Professor Amos Dolbear of Tufts University and author Hamlin Garland become the chief investigators.

1892—George Pellew, an associate of the ASPR, is killed in an accident, and on March 22, 1892, begins to communicate with Dr. Richard Hodgson through Leonore Piper. Pellew (given the pseudonym "George Pelham") gradually takes over as Piper's primary control from Phinuit. Hodgson abandons the secondary personality hypothesis and adopts the spirit hypothesis based on Pellew's very distinct personality coming through at the sittings.

1894—Professor Oliver Lodge, Frederic W. H. Myers, and Dr. Charles Richet of France investigate the mediumship of Eusapia Palladino of Italy, concluding that she is a "mixed" medium, producing some real phenomena but occasionally cheating.

1898—Frederic W. H. Myers has the first of over 150 sittings with British trance medium Rosalie Thompson. Myers becomes convinced of the spirit hypothesis.

1901—Frederic W. H. Myers dies and soon begins communicating with Professor Oliver Lodge through medium Rosalie Thompson. Over the next few years, Myers communicates through other mediums and offers what come to be known as the cross-correspondences.

1903—*Human Personality and Its Survival of Bodily Death*, a 416-page book begun but not completely finished by Frederic W. H. Myers before his death, is completed by others and is published. It becomes the seminal work in the field.

1905—Dr. Richard Hodgson dies and soon begins communicating through Leonore Piper, the medium he had studied for eighteen years.

1906—Because of Hodgson's death, the ASPR is reorganized and becomes the American Institute for Scientific Research under the direction of Dr. James H. Hyslop, formerly a professor of logic and ethics at Columbia University. The ASPR becomes a branch of the Institute. After Hyslop's death in 1920, it becomes the Boston Society for Psychic Research. In 1941, it is reintegrated into the ASPR with headquarters in New York.

1907—Dr. James H. Hyslop begins investigating the mediumship of "Mrs. Chenoweth."

1909—*The Survival of Man* by Sir Oliver Lodge is published.

1914—The mediumship of Pearl Curran, a St. Louis, Missouri. housewife through whom an entity known as Patience Worth communicates volumes of wisdom, is investigated by many researchers.

1915—Sir Oliver Lodge begins receiving messages from his son Raymond, killed on the battlefield in France. Many of the messages come through Gladys Osborne Leonard, a trance medium. In 1916, Sir Oliver's book,

Raymond or Life and Death is published and reaches a wide audience.

1917—Rev. Charles Drayton Thomas, a SPR member, begins sitting with Gladys Osborne Leonard, receiving many evidential messages from his deceased father and sister. The book and newspaper tests are developed providing evidence that the information communicated does not come by means of telepathy.

1925—Sir William Barrett dies and begins sending messages to his wife, Lady Barrett, a physician and dean of a women's medical school, through the mediumship of Leonore Piper and Gladys Osborne Leonard.

1940—Sir Oliver Lodge, last of the "champions" of psychical research, dies.

Bibliography

Barrett, Sir William. 1917. *On the Threshold of the Unseen.* New York: E. P. Dutton & Co.

——————. [1926] 1986. *Death-Bed Vision.* 3rd ed. Northamptonshire, England: The Aquarian Press.

Barrett, Lady Florence. 1937. *Personality Survives Death.* , London: Longmans, Green and Co.

Berger, Arthur S. and Joyce. 1991. *The Encyclopedia of Parapsychology and Psychical Research.* Paragon House.

Bond, Frederick Bligh. 1918.*The Gate of Remembrance.* Oxford: B. H. Blackwell.

——————. 1919. *The Hill of Vision.* London: Constable & Co., Ltd.

Burton, Jean. 1944. *Heyday of a Wizard: Daniel Home, the Medium.* New York: Alfred A. Knopf.

Chambers, John. 1998. *Conversations with Eternity: The Forgotten Masterpiece of Victor Hugo.* Boca Raton: New Paradigm Books.

Crookes, Sir William. [1906] 1922. *Researches into the Phenomena of Modern Spiritualism.* 4th ed. Los Angeles: Austin Publishing Co.

Cummins, Geraldine. 1932. *The Road to Immortality.* London: The Aquarian Publishing Co.

——————. 1951. *Unseen Adventures.* London: Rider and Company.

Doyle, Arthur Conan. *The Vital Message.* New York: George H. Doran Company.

—————. 1926. *The History of Spiritualism*. New York: George H. Doran Company.

Eddy, Sherwood. 1954. *You Will Survive Death*. The Omega Press, Surrey, England, 1954

Edmonds, I. G. 1978. *D. D. Home: The Man Who Talked with Ghosts*. Nashville/New York: Thomas Nelson Inc.

Fortune, Dion. 1986. *Glastonbury*. Northamptonshire, England: The Aquarian Press.

Gardner, Martin. 1998. *The Wreck of the Titanic Foretold?* Amherst, N.Y.: Prometheus Books.

Garland, Hamlin. 1908. *The Shadow World*. New York: Harper & Brothers Publishers.

—————. 1936. *Forty Years of Psychic Research*. New York: The MacMillan Co.

—————. 1939. *The Mystery of the Buried Crosses*. New York: E. P. Dutton and Company.

Harding, Emma. [1869] 1970. *Modern American Spiritualism*. New Hyde Park, N.Y.: University Books.

Hare, Robert, M. D. 1855. *Experimental Investigation of the Spirit Manifestations*. New York: Partridge & Brittan.

Holt, Henry. 1914. *On the Cosmic Relations*. Boston and New York: Houghton Mifflin Company.

Home, Daniel D. [1862] n.d. *Incidents in My Life*. Secaucus, N.J.: University Books, Inc.

Hyslop, James H. 1919. *Contact with the Other World*. New York: The Century Co.

Josephson, Matthew. 1942. *Victor Hugo*. Garden City, N.Y.: Doubleday, Doran & Co., Inc.

Kardec, Allan. [1857] n.d. *The Spirits' Book*. Mexico: Amapse Society.

—————. [1874] n.d. *The Book on Mediums*. York Beach, Maine: Samuel Weiser, Inc.

Kenawell, William W. 1965. *The Quest at Glastonbury*. New York: Garrett Publications.

Kelway-Bamber, L. [1919] n.d. *Claude's Book*. London: Psychic Book Club.

Leonard, Gladys Osborne. 1931. *My Life in Two Worlds*. London: Cassell & Company, Ltd.

Litvag, Irving. 1972. *Singer in the Shadows*. New York: The MacMillan Co.

Lodge, Oliver. 1909. *The Survival of Man*. New York: Moffat, Yard and Co.

————. 1916. *Raymond or Life and Death*. New York: George H. Doran Company.

———— . 1932. *Past Years*. New York: Charles Scribner's Sons.

Medhurst, R. G. 1972. *Crookes and the Spirit World*. New York: Taplinger Publishing Co.

Moore, R. Laurence. 1977. *In Search of White Crows*. New York: Oxford University Press.

Moses, William Stainton. [1924] 1976. *Spirit Teachings*. New York: Arno Press.

————. *More Spirit Teachings. Meilach.com*

Mowbray, Jay Henry. 1998. *Sinking of the Titanic Eyewitness Accounts*. Mineola, N.Y.: Dover Publication, Inc.

Myers, F. W. H. [1903] 1961. *Human Personality and its Survival of Bodily Death*. New Hyde Park, N.Y.: University Books, Inc.

Pressing, R. G. c. 1938. *Rappings that Startled the World*. Lily Dale N.Y.: Dale News.

Prince, Walter Franklin. [1927] 1964. *The Case of Patience Worth*. New Hyde Park, N.Y.: University Books.

Robbins, Anne Manning. 1909. *Both Sides of the Veil*. Boston: Sherman, French & Co.

Smith, Eleanor Touhey. 1968. *Psychic People*. New York: William Morrow & Co., Inc.

Stead, William T. [1909] n.d. *After Death or Letters from Julia*. Kessinger Publishing.

Stockton, Frank R. (through the hand of Etta De Camp). 1913. *Return of Frank R. Stockton*. New York: William Rider & Sons, Ltd.

Thomas, Charles Drayton. [1922] 1948. *Some New Evidence for Human Survival*. London: Spiritualist Press Ltd.

Travers Smith, Hester. 1919. *Voices from the Void*. New York: E. P. Dutton & Company.

Tweedale, Charles L. 1925. *Man's Survival After Death*. London: Psychic Book Club.

Wallace, Alfred Russel. 1896. *Miracles and Modern Spiritualism*. London: George Redway.

Wickland, Carl A. [1924] 1974. *Thirty Years Among the Dead*. Newcastle Publishing Co., Inc.

—————. 1934. *The Gateway of Understanding*. Los Angeles: National Psychological Institute, Inc.

Winocour, Jack. 1960. *The Story of The Titanic*. New York: Dover Publications, Inc.

Woodman, Pardoe, and Estelle Stead. 1970. *The Blue Island*. London: Hutchinson & Co.,

Worth, Patience. 1917. *The Sorry Tale*. New York: Henry Holt & Co.

Yost, Casper, S. 1916. *Patience Worth*. New York: Henry Holt & Co.

To order additional copies of this book,
please send full amount plus $5.00 for
postage and handling for the first book and
$1.00 for each additional book.
Minnesota residents add 7.125 percent sales tax

Send orders to:

Galde Press
PO Box 460
Lakeville, Minnesota 55044-0460

Credit card orders call 1–800–777–3454
Fax (952) 891–6091
Visit our website at *www.galdepress.com*
and download our free catalog,
or write for our catalog.

CPSIA information can be obtained
at www.ICGtesting.com
Printed in the USA
LVHW100300190622
721593LV00003B/97